Lincoln In The White House

Lincoln In The White House

a play

Robert Manns

*The playwright is a Member
of the Dramatists Guild
of America, Inc.*

Writers Club Press
New York   Lincoln   Shanghai

Lincoln In The White House

Writers Club Press
an imprint of iUniverse, Inc.

For information address:
iUniverse
2021 Pine Lake Road, Suite 100
Lincoln, NE 68512
www.iuniverse.com

ISBN: 0-595-20910-6 (Pbk)
ISBN: 0-595-74516-4 (Cloth)

Printed in the United States of America

To
Dikran Tulaine

Contents

"A people without history is not redeemed from time, for history is a pattern of timeless moments."

—T.S. Eliot
Little Gidding, Section V

A Note on the Verse

In his treatise on poetry and form in A Note on War Poetry, T.S. Eliot really does, for me, close the book on questions about the substance of poetry and form.

Poetry is the manner in which we regard something. Form is its shape.

Poetry can be figured in simile, rhythm, metaphor, symbol, sign, assonance, dissonance, and other means of play like rime.

Form can be given by line length, representational shape (concrete), even the number of letters or spaces per line.

But one thing is sure: Poetry and form are two different things since there is surely imagistic or poetic writing in prose forms, i.e. the novel, short story and letters. And there is form that breathes nothing of poetry whatsoever, as in the work of many rimers whose metrical stories are pure, and often comic, narrations. The limerick, for instance, has no wish to be poetry but hews to a form that provides surprise (also present in poetry) and fun.

LINCOLN IN THE WHITE HOUSE is a verse play concentrated in decasyllabic lines often possessing no real poetic content but generating definite rhythms within the contained line. These sectors are mainly informational or transitional and I can think of no reason to labor an audience with figurative imagery here. Poetry does (hopefully) occur when emotions are being spent because figurative language is being employed here toward heightened emotional involvement. Eliot's Cocktail Party, for instance, is surely a play in accentual verse contributing to a mood one might call poetry, but it is not written in figurative language at all.

Christopher Fry, on the other hand, employing a spirit and density of images not seen since the Elizabethans, goes figurative in accentual fives.

Syllabic line counts are nothing new, of course. Dylan Thomas's Ballad of the Long Legged Bait is a classic example of a ballad in nines. But syllabic measurement may be new to drama. I simply don't know of another usage of it there, and it affords freedoms other metrics make difficult or impossible. At any rate, it is my choice and I hope it works for the audiences of my time.

Besides being a solid and beautifully written drama, LINCOLN is a moving and authentic piece. Its dramatization will contribute much to a better understanding of the most tragic and the most important episode in the history of the American Nation.

Bell I. Wiley, Professor of History
Emory University, Atlanta, Georgia

Cast

CLARA, a tavern waitress
THOMAS DYER, a young man
ABRAHAM LINCOLN, President of the United States
SEWARD, Secretary of State in the north
WILLIE LINCOLN, Lincoln's son
MARY LINCOLN, wife of the President of the north
ROBERT E. LEE, Commander of the Army of Virginia
McCLELLAN, Commander of the Army of the Potomac
STANTON, northern Secretary of War
COLONEL TAYLOR, Lee's adutant
PAUL, ALFRED, MOTHER JOHN, and other Southern soldiers
GRANT, new commander of the Army of The Potomac
RAWLINGS, Grant's aide
MEADE, General
EMILIE HELM, a southern wife, Mary Lincoln's sister
A KITTEN, or reasonable facsimile
ELIZABETH KECKLEY, Mary Lincoln's servant
TWO PINKERTON MEN
MRS. HARVEY, a solicitor
YOUNG MAN, a soldier
WOMAN, a solicitor

Preface

Lincoln In The White House is the single play formulation from **Lincoln, Part I** and **Lincoln, Part II**, published by iUniverse. The latter begun in two-part form when the author was in his thirties were discontinued for years. Now, consistent with the time we live in toward miniaturation, the plays are in one part. Finally. The cast has been halved and, to cure an observation by Christopher Fry, the play has been made "exportable." *we dope.*

AM

SCENE I

A Washington, D.C. tavern. Tom Dyer, a young man, and Clara, a waitress. Clara present. Enter Dyer. Clara is setting a table and humming to herself when Dyer enters.

CLARA: Well, if it isn't Tom Dyer. You've been gone at least a week.

DYER: Two, Clara. I've been in Georgia, where it's actually warm this time of year. Hot on one day. But warm as the people are, they're still cool-headed. Cold as it gets here in Washington the tempers are hot; how's that?

CLARA: Search me.

DYER: I didn't meet anyone with a temper like yours, for instance.

CLARA: I don't have a temper.

DYER: Right, and I came in here on wheels, not feet.

CLARA: Not much of one, anyway.

DYER: I'm a very observant and independent man.

CLARA: I wouldn't know, I've yet to meet one.

DYER: Clara, let me tell you something. I just shook Lincoln's sturdy hand while he was on the way to the inauguration and, I tell you, no one has a better grip who isn't part bear. His hand swallowed mine whole. I think if we don't understand him yet, we can blame his measurements; there is too much man.

CLARA: When was this?

DYER: Minutes ago.

CLARA: You shook his hand?!

DYER: I did.

CLARA: That's worth a drink on me. *(Calling to a bartender)* Henry, an ale for this kid!

DYER: That will make me drunk.

CLARA: So get drunk. You must have been halfway there anyway to get so close to Lincoln.

DYER: Well, I get carried away, I admit, but I wasn't drunk. When I saw him coming, I saw a face of tragedy and strength I've never seen before. I jumped on his carriage and extended my hand. He took it, Clara! Then the police broke me away and I ran 'til I was run out and made for here.

CLARA: Well, when did you take to Lincoln, Tom?

DYER: I never have, but he impressed me.

CLARA: I hope his army impresses you.

DYER: No, I don't think it does.

CLARA: Well, have you read the papers? War seems the only answer and you're the age.

DYER: I know, but there are two sides to fight on.

CLARA: Oh, no sooner will Lincoln kiss the Capitol stairs than this tyke, this spoon clutcher, will undo his bib for the South. I'll get your ale.

(Exit Clara)

DYER: Hey, they've got the great Southern general, Robert Lee, down there. Who have we got? We? Who's we? I'm confused.

(Enter Clara)

CLARA: *(Setting down the ale)* D'you know who you'll be fighting? Your own friends, your own neighbors, Tom.

DYER: My girl's in Georgia.

CLARA: So? My uncle is in Tennessee.

DYER: I asked Patricia! She said that if I hated her and loved all her slaves she thought I should take up arms here. Or if I would have slaves be just slaves and loved her beyond doubt, she thought I would bear arms, and so I will, for her and for Southern rights. It was a choice.

CLARA: What real lady could reject all that? What a crock! Romantic doggerel!

DYER: I thought you had no temper.

CLARA: So you were wrong!

DYER: I couldn't choose by reason. I reached for it.

CLARA:—and got taken in, you fool! Why, you just shook Lincoln's hand!

DYER: Right, I shook it.

CLARA: So, it means nothing?

DYER: I'm in love, Clara. I'm designed for love—look at me. I'm made for it!

CLARA: Well, be in love, but let Lincoln lead you! This war, this war that's almost here, what's it really about, anyway? Is it slavery?

DYER: Oh, there's slavery in it, I know, and I'm against yoking any man to another against his will.

CLARA: Well?

DYER: Well.

CLARA: Well, go to war, then.

DYER: *(Standing and throwing down coins)* I will, but I'll pay my own way, Clara sweet.

CLARA: *(As he exits)* It's not cowboys and Indians, Tom, its ugly war. Think about it.

Scene 2

A room of the White House. Present Mary Lincoln.

MARY: Well, Mr. Seward, though I'm no judge of it,
    I'm inclined to think our President
    made his inaugural address sound firm.
    His speech was not moderate, nor was it
    radical, but raced in that direction
    of the well thought point driven hard, you know.
    I was quite satisfied with its tenor.

SEWARD: So was I, Mary, but he modified me,
    on my word, more heavily than weight
    would allow when he addressed the Southern states,
    asking temperance and a conclusion
    far more peaceful than the one they pursue.

MARY: I'm told he used your better figures whole.

SEWARD: Oh, no Ma'm, not likely did he do that
    or anywhere nearby. He razored me.
    I submit, it will be timorous work
    making a strong leader of old Lincoln,
    but I'm pledged to it, devil take me.
    That's my position, dear Mary, what's yours?

MARY: As our General Scott has made plans for,
    a knot, sir, around their necks. Full armadas
    on all seas around their shores, estuaries
    and all ports, breaking off trade in cotton,

their lifeblood. His anaconda will feed
on Southern frigates and merchant vessels.

SEWARD: His note to the South has been ignored
of his intention to supply the fort
that chokes the waters of Charleston Harbor
and has given them first cause of a kind.
That note, Mary, was a heavy gauntlet.
The glove was thrown down with fist intact.
I wish I had amended it some.

MARY: But, William, he never asked you to.

SEWARD: True,
that's the trouble.

MARY: Well, what heaven has borne
earth must have a use for, do you think so?
Your use at present, it seems, is given
to waiting and humble supplication
for that office tendered you by Lincoln.

SEWARD: My use at present is a humpback whale
without a tail, rudderless, lost at sea,
and wondering what's next.

MARY: Next is service,
since it is a law of human nature
that those same bonds of concord uniting men,
once broken, can do quick strangulation
on us all. Serve the man, Seward, serve him.

SEWARD: I swear I must go think him over again;
    Good afternoon.

(Exit Seward)

MARY: *(Mumbling)* Love our politicians.

(Enter Willie, Lincoln's son)

WILLIE: Is my father president everywhere?

MARY: No Willie, just of his United States
    and they are his because he is first man
    in them. Even your brother Tad knows that.
    Although they're not too well united now.

WILLIE: Well, Mother, I thought he was president
    everywhere. Shall I give up the idea
    that we own England?

MARY: Oh, stifle the thought.
    You'll earn a visit from the English navy,
    and history will be lectured you
    at national expense. Do forget it.

(Enter Lincoln)

LINCOLN: Well, what's amiss that there is no wreckage,
    not one Mohawk, no Blackfeet, warriors
    ringing the rooms in piercing hunting cries
    or thundering horseless down our dark halls?
    I commend your good keep of him, Mary.

WILLIE: Father, what is war?

LINCOLN: It is armed argument
   and I will hope we do not have it.

MARY: Our Willie is a wisp of tendril
   Abe, anchoring him to a life itself: I worry.

LINCOLN: There's reason to believe, Wife, that our god
   preserves the frail when they are valued sons.

MARY: Just the same, I believe he should be watched more closely.

LINCOLN: We'll continue, then.

WILLIE: Sir, who owns England?

LINCOLN: Why, I guess the English.

WILLIE: I think you do.

LINCOLN: How's that, Willie?

WILLIE: Mr. Seward says so.

LINCOLN: Well, I think not. It is true England thinks
   the North unfair against our Southern states
   but she will not interfere. Owning England,
   as you put it, is out of the question.
   In truth, this ownership is poor language.
   I serve a country. I don't own so much
   as the house we live in. So much for that
   vanity.

WILLIE: May I go to my room now?

LINCOLN: You may.

(Exit Willie)

LINCOLN: And may I, dear Mary, summon
   your interest a moment toward a new fear
   I seem to be raising like a shipwreck
   from my sleep. I am so vulnerable
   as president to insult, injury,
   attack even, that I begin to sense
   an uneasiness about our persons.
   Last week my viewpoint on slave extension
   earned me three letters, two from our deep South,
   that promised attacks for my insolence.
   Once more mankind will kill for mere belief.
   Thinking urges him to it. Thought inflamed.
   My God, how quickly can we make the leap
   from thinker to murder, rape, massacre
   and whole war. In minutes, to damnation!

MARY: Please, Abe, you turn hopefulness to fear
   with talk like this. It closes on my heart
   in terror. Your office demands courage,
   Sir, courage and the will of the Fisher.

LINCOLN: I'll devote my animal will to it.

MARY: That relieves me. Next, you have not seen my dress
   for the ball.

LINCOLN: I thought that was forbidden.

MARY: Oh, is it?

LINCOLN: Yes, by custom or something.

MARY: I like to think you may initiate
   new practices, not tow behind the old.
   You are President, Abe; I am your proud wife.

LINCOLN: Our issue is clearly a civil war
   with no time to give to its circumvention.
   I am a boardinghouse keeper too kept
   with taking in guests to fight the fire
   at the house's other end. Figure that, will you?
   So, where is this ball's eventful dress, then?

MARY: I reconsider. You have had too much
   too soon for your years.

LINCOLN: Why, this is coquetry.
   You last played it on that happy day
   You took me in for your vanquished husband.

MARY: Tush, you're a vain man, Abe, but vow
   if I never loved you at our marriage
   I have grown used to your egotism
   and do love you now, professed openly.
   The way forward is strewn with buttercups.

LINCOLN: I took you by natural selection.

You were plump and I lanky as timber.
Our children, I reasoned, would fall between.

MARY: You may go to the ball with the cook, sir.

LINCOLN: Lincoln's head and heart tells Lincoln's arms
   he wants his wife. *(They embrace)*

MARY: Do we fight to love, Abe?

LINCOLN: Well, here comes Seward on a tear.

(Enter Seward)

SEWARD: Lincoln,
   its done. The rebels have possessed Fort Sumter.
   This bodes war; war takes troops! Where have we any?

LINCOLN: Mister Seward, I'd be much obliged
   for your escort to Mrs. Lincoln.
   She has work in our rooms.

SEWARD: I'll do it, then,
   but I've yet to get accustomed to your moods.

(Exit Seward and Mary Lincoln, enter Willie opposite)

WILLIE: Shouting woke me. There are men in the street.

LINCOLN: My much loved son, it's a monkey heyday
   wherein all tree chattering counts as reason,
   excitement nips at good Aristotle's wings,

and our quiet streets are made jungle paths
dark to the sun and untrespassable.
It is a case of barbershop thinking
where, as the hair falls, so goes reputation,
logic, precaution, the mental gymnastic
of our learning and our jurisprudence,
wisdom's extremities. Man barbers man,
therefore, to fight, to which he proudly goes
no hair, no reason, notwithstanding.
It is primitive and sad, this impulse.
That boy-that boy, Dyer, who greeted me
at my coach, the day of my inaugural ball.
Why are sunless thoughts on him now?

*(Exit Lincoln and Willie, enter opposite McClellan and Stanton,
McClellan with a roll of maps)*

STANTON: Our Cameron is the most peaceable
and easygoing war's secretary
we could cling to. Why's he kept, McClellan?
While he stays, the South arms itself with Lee.

MCCLELLAN: Stanton, while Lincoln ignores your knowledge,
your stature, he will browse my field maps
as though he were learning to wage whole wars.

STANTON: You have every reason to make complaint
of his nosing in, but he covers you well,
result of his exceeding length, you know.

MCCLELLAN: True, he is long.

STANTON: Long, he's extended, George!
   Lincoln is a most extensive fellow.
   His Cro-Magnon features and yardstick gait
   take him back deep into time. Lincoln
   is the original gorilla! Note,
   however, he has the foot of a longspur.

MCCLELLAN: That's true, too, he rattles my every effort.
   Preparations a sore in his ear.
   If I say I want ten thousand more men,
   he says I am Richmond's owner now
   and all I need do is foreclose its mortgage.

STANTON: He's done all his fighting in the circuit courts,
   that's plain. What's this? I'm a whipped dog, he's here!

(Enter Lincoln)

MCCLELLAN: Mr. President, I never heard you knock!

LINCOLN: I never knocked is why, General. And
   I rarely do in my own domicile

STANTON: Well, you heard our discussion then, sir?

LINCOLN: No, Mr. Stanton, do you think I should have?

MCCLELLAN: No!

STANTON: Yes, yes, Mr. Lincoln; I confirm
   the General's reaction to that, surely.
   We were on the person of Cameron

whose office we both were admiring
for its henny neatness and efficiency.

LINCOLN: True, Stanton—true; it was a feathered bed.

STANTON: No, I meant it in good faith, sir, very neat.
But you say "was". Is that indicative
of some change? If so, I will protest to you
against any foe he has, on my word.

LINCOLN: Well, sir, let us first strike a bargain
not to throw fish at the mongers of fish
lest, in time, we hunger—since we know well
that any man close to hunger, far from pride,
will eat whatever he's had set before him.

STANTON: That was long, but I think I master it.

LINCOLN: I read once of a man in our country
who had such regard for the unadorned truth
he spent most of his time, good Stanton,
embellishing it. Cameron is appointed
to Russia.

STANTON: I didn't know he knew Russian
but hopes he knows their climate. I wish him well.
Who's to succeed?

LINCOLN: I think an able man.

STANTON: Ah?

LINCOLN: A man of good experience, too.

STANTON: I hope a man with some fire in him
    to discharge his duties ably and fast.

LINCOLN: Yes, speed is his and important, also.
    But diligence being his stamp and color,
    I think I was more persuaded by that.

STANTON: Well, I will leave you to your General,
    Mr. Lincoln. My office calls for hard work;
    I extend my hand.

LINCOLN: Then, on your way home
    you might care to look in at the War Department,
    see what's required, would you, Stanton?

MCCLELLAN: Him, Mr. President?

STANTON: I must sit down;
    no, I must not. There's work enough for Caesar,
    Hannibal, and Old James the King in one.
    Lincoln, I am grateful.

MCCLELLAN: Where are you going?

STANTON: Going? I am going to make Abe Lincoln
    President of these United States!

(Exit Stanton)

(Enter Stanton)

STANTON: McClellan, no more throwing fish, you hear?
  It's a war food and not to be dispensed
  with casualness!

(Exit Stanton)

MCCLELLAN: I am shocked by it.

LINCOLN: So is Stanton, George. Next, your own strategy
  is quite unknown to me and that flies
  in the face of our losing the command
  of Robert Lee to the South, a dead loss
  we have to overcome by being prudent,
  resourceful, and, above all, well charted.
  He will test us. So, then, down to your plans.

MCCLELLAN: Sir, my plans are immature and not down.

LINCOLN: But they must be. Plans that are not down
  are up, and plans in the air are not plans.
  We must lay down something.

MCCLELLAN: I'm all afield.
  I have only a notion for striking Richmond.

LINCOLN: Well, we must have a plan for it
  within the month. And I must say to you
  that action must come out of the egg
  before all dies intact.

MCCLELLAN: Egg? There is none.

LINCOLN: Then you must lay one, George. Good news is ours
    from the West. An unknown General,
    one Grant by name, laid out two forts by quick siege
    and, having demolished the door, now threatens
    one whole side of our rebel states house.
    Our western armies are restlessly engaged,
    our eastern one, yours, now harbors notions.
    This will not do. I ask you into action.

MCCLELLAN: As asking is ordering, I will comply.
    My thoughts were on this route to Richmond
    there to take Lee's rear in quick surprise.
    I will ask for forty-thousand troops more.

LINCOLN: That should make you near two hundred thousand.

MCCLELLAN: And still outnumbered.

LINCOLN: Really?
    We'll support you.

MCCLELLAN: I'll plan now for it.

LINCOLN: Success attend you, sir.

    (Drums)

SCENE 3

Lee and Taylor. Sporadic small weapons fire.

LEE: McClellan's batteries are removed and gone,
    Colonel Taylor. I could not keep the squirrel
    from its tree and so we lose the kill.
    The hunt is over and army's fled.
    Bitter, bitter loss. The war might have ended
    here and many deaths been averted.

TAYLOR: Sir, it is not your fault. Your generals
    failed you ten times if once. Your whole design
    of battle got piecemeal play all week.
    Seven whole days watched them sport afield
    like lion cubs in African plains.
    If one was not late to get engaged,
    the other was absent. When one marched fast,
    another got lost. It was as though
    they had all slept with each other's wives
    and would not be found side by side.
    Why are you scratching your head, sir?

LEE: I have an itch.

TAYLOR: Let me see, General.
    Why, you have a tick, Sir, hold yourself still.
    There you are, a Northern fellow, I guess,
    wanting to pick your brains. I'll make him an ash.

LEE: What's from the west?

TAYLOR: Our circlement's complete.
      The Union Navy took New Orleans
      and now sits on all the waters 'round us.

LEE: That is Scott's Anaconda, Colonel,
      hugging us for joy. We must win quick now
      or bleed to death. Next stop, Washington.

SCENE 4

Washington. Same room of the White House. Mary at a window,
Lincoln standing.

MARY: Now, Abe, what shall we do, losing Willie
    and a stable of horses the same night,
    one to the fever, the other fire? What, sir—?
    God is taking sons, sons, Mr. Lincoln!

LINCOLN: There is nothing for us to do Mary,
    but recover from our life's longest night.
    I am frozen in a land of disbelief
    and am finding life itself damnable.
    Willie gone as though so much horse flesh.
    I say it is contemptible of life!
    It is like the fire was meant to frame him!

MARY: There was no cause for it in my mind.

LINCOLN: No, none, and there is no court held for it,
    either. It is just what we inherit
    of an inexplicable and tawdry life.
    And so it goes.

MARY: I hate the way it goes.

LINCOLN: Willie is adrift in the tides, Mary,
    and unrecoverable. The clamshell
    emptied, carapace of crab, beached seaworm
    are all Willie and the gulls will sing him

through eternity. His fever is out   '
with the ebbing waters of an ocean,
I tell you, and we must not drown him in us.
The stabled horses, his favorite pony,
likewise assumed his final agony
and festered end. That is as we have it.
No more, no more is there to this extreme.
You must try to take our loss more lightly.
We have a raging war on our doorstep.

MARY: And what if we should lose?

LINCOLN: Perish the thought.

MARY: But they are in close-by country, you know.

LINCOLN: Hanged if I don't. I hear about it hourly.
    They are as close as our loss of Willie.
    Our army, instead of defeating Lee,
    apologized for its presence in his front,
    curtsied, demurred and flew to cover.
    We are behaving as though we're bad boys
    and have no business in the field with men.

MARY: I want to stay to hear the reports,
    if you don't mind.

LINCOLN: I do mind, of course. What now?

MARY: I wish to stay.

LINCOLN: I wish you would not, though.

(Rises, goes to her at the window)
Yonder building, Mary, is asylum
for souls tortured to various degrees
as we now are. But there they have no control
over greater magnitude of their thoughts.
Delirium and excess are encouraged
in the small hope that devil will out
and host be delivered. I want you here,
not there. You have our children to rear.
Are you clear of it, pet?

MARY: I think so now.

(Exit Mary)

(Lincoln returns to his desk)

LICOLN: This war between our states has all but turned
       me under, and may yet accomplish that.
       Can the stronger arm lose to the weaker?
       Can the richer purse lose to the poorer?
       England will have a great laugh over this,
       her sympathies are for the South. She knows
       that the stronger heart can take it all.
       The name Dyer comes on me now, why so?

(Enter Seward)

SEWARD: My god, Sir, you have my heartfelt sympathies
       for your losses last night. Unexpected
       grief is greatest always as surprise joy
       is and I wish I could share your deep pain.

LINCOLN: Thank you, Seward, Mary and I are crushed
by it. It was an avalanche attended
by tornado and will take some time
to dress our sorrow and wear garlands.
Tell me, do we still have Vicksburg locked tight?

SEWARD: She's under siege by land and water, Sir.

LINCOLN: Well, unless she can escape by an act
of transcendence, she should be ours by now,
don't you think?

SEWARD: It should be, Mr. Lincoln.

LINCOLN: I am worried, Seward.

SEWARD: So am I, Sir,
ripped by sad dissension, torn by fighting,
we stumble and bluff our way toward brute death
like children in a ghastly nightmare.
It is pitiful to consider us.
Lee has just turned himself to Gettysburg.

LINCOLN: Good grief, our army's there.

SEWARD: You're on edge, sir.
It's there for that reason, combat, you know.
Let experience be your teacher now
and hope your guide. I think if we stop them
it must be at Gettysburg.

LINCOLN: So I fear.

SEWARD: There is nothing now to do but hang on.

LINCOLN: Oh, I hate hanging, Seward.

SEWARD: Would you like chess?

LINCOLN: I am too depressed to play at checkers.

(Lincoln goes to window)

LINCOLN: My time never seems given to endings.
     I may be the very flux embracing
     this entire nation, Seward, and my end
     would signal the end of flux, misery
     and engagement, but I hope I am not
     that instrumental.

SEWARD: Have been and will be.
     Your giving the Potomac army to Meade
     has provided us more strength in the east
     and at least a small waterway of chance
     against Lee. I make it sound nautical
     but that's the armada I sense coming.
     Nor am I giddy. Your job done, you watch.

LINCOLN: Upon my life, is that all?

SEWARD: No more than that.

LINCOLN: And wait the result.

SEWARD: And wait the result.

LINCOLN: I'll watch for the morning messenger.
   That is a play, I think, on mourning, Seward?

SCENE 5

The field, west of, and approaching, Gettysburg. Lee with telescope, and Taylor. Small weapon fire.

LEE: That way lies Gettysburg, Colonel Taylor.
    It is a shame of nature that men despoil
    such fertile land with war. What do you think,
    would you live here?

TAYLOR: I might, Sir, if I had to.

LEE: Had to! That's being prisoner to it.

TAYLOR: That's the provision by which I would live here.
    I prefer my mountains and deep foothills
    to tabletop ground. It's curious.

LEE: Why is it curious?

TAYLOR: I prefer, by far,
    the same of women.

LEE: Quite, Colonel,
    you will drive the horses hereabouts mad.
    Now, can you guess what's in store for this army?

TAYLOR: Nossir, I cannot, and if I could,
    I should outrank you and be in command.

LEE: *(Laughs)*

Well, I think we will whip them and failing that,
they will whip us. Their new commander, Meade,
will make no blunders, you may count on it.
Our spirits are high, and fight is spoiled for
by every member in these joyous ranks;
and though we will be outnumbered again,
the union numbers have not taken toll
lately. I think we may end this war here,
if God is willing.

TAYLOR: I pray so, General.

LEE: For my part, I am well satisfied
     with the busy joy among our sparrows.
     The cooks and foragers, those rufous towhees,
     have provided us with good sustenance
     and even the blackbirds are kept employed,
     every non-commissioned officer
     is a noisy jay full of hop and piping,
     the brigades are led by plummeting hawks.
     Now our eagles, Longstreet, Hill, and Ewell,
     should be fight thirsty and blood hungry,
     tight alert and in their best readiness.
     I could be more content with larger flocks,
     Colonel, but there are no better ones.

TAYLOR: Yes sir. There is a soldier coming up here
     and I am due at the quartermaster.

LEE: I don't know him, and he is out of ranks.

TAYLOR: Halt! Your full name and commander!

(Enter Dyer, who halts)

DYER: Private Thomas Dyer, Sir, of General Longstreet's Corps.

TAYLOR: What are you doing here, Private Dyer?

DYER: I came to see General Lee, Sir. I have a message.

LEE: Go, Colonel. The private will keep me company
   'til you return.

TAYLOR: Yessir.

(Exit Taylor)

DYER: I have heard General Longstreet two times say he does
   not agree with this.

LEE: Well, agree with what?

DYER: Facing the enemy directly.

LEE: But it would be harder yet to face them
   indirectly. What do you think he means?

DYER: He will oppose your plans.

LEE: You are telling me you heard this from him?

DYER: Yessir. I had brought his aide some rations and heard
   him from his tent.

LEE: Well, you have had a bad nightmare, I think.
    That will put you in serious trouble
    with your general, if he hears it.

DYER: General Lee, I serve under you.

LEE: Nossir, you do not. You serve Mister Longstreet
    who serves under me. You are first obliged
    to him. Were he to deny you heard him,
    you could be court-martialed promptly.

DYER: Sir, I swear—

LEE: To swear
    is not a good Christian vocation,
    if you understand me so well you will
    have dreamt it.

DYER: Nossir, I heard it—

LEE: I know you did not, am I clear?

DYER: General Lee—

LEE: Here comes my adjutant, who prosecutes
    storytellers out of school. No more, please.

    (Enter the adjutant)

DYER: Sir, I've failed you.

LEE: What's the word of Stuart's cavalry, Colonel?

(Exit Dyer)

TAYLOR: None, Sir.

LEE: They will be out of this conflict then,
    and it is some loss. For now, let's encamp.

SCENE 6

Scene is the White House. Lincoln is sitting, reading. Tad is listening.

LINCOLN: The Greeks told more stories than we tell truth
    nowadays, Tad, and we are truthful people
    by and large, we think. This is one of them:
    there was a maiden named Atalanta
    whose boyish face of purest olive light
    one day was hung with clouds of abject fear.
    Her fortune told of ruin should she marry
    and she fled her suitors. Men hunted her,
    as men will do. Thus, she informed them:
    I will be prize to him who conquers me
    in running here to there, *(designating*
    some far hill, a distance best only set
    for runners of the rarest skill and wind).
    Many tried, nonetheless, losing their races
    in quickest order. She was too fast.
    Her judge in these contests was Hippomenes,
    a handsome youth, lately come enamored
    of his mistress, who one day stepped forward
    and announced his wish to run. "No," she said,
    having some fondness for his handsome aspect.
    He persisted, knowing he should win.
    Hippomenes had visited his goddess
    Venus and the two planned mutually
    a small trick to give victory to the boy.
    Well, then, the race began; Atalanta
    streaked to the front, Hippomenes watching
    her agile form and lovely color.

He threw down something, Atalanta
turning to see a golden apple.
She returned to marvel at the comely fruit.
So Hippomenes, in his turn, led the race.
She caught him quickly *(women left behind*
are prone to great exertion) and she tore bye.
A second golden apple brought her back
again, and again Hippomenes
assumed the lead. Once more, too, was he caught
and at the instant of her passing
he discharged his final golden apple.
She deplored the trick but stopped anyway, reasoning that
two apples were one short of enough for a whole pie and had
never much liked the wasting of good food, when it was all
confessed.

TAD: So, but then what happened to her fortune?

LINCOLN: Cybele turned them both to pussy cats,
    as I remember.

(Enter Mary Lincoln)

MARY: What book have you there, Abe?

LINCOLN: Bulfinch, edited by Lincoln, Mary.

MARY: What is Bulfinch?

LINCOLN: Why, a book of Greek myths.

MARY: Do I know it?

LINCOLN: I presume you don't.
  It is safe for Tad if altered a bit.
  It was first published a few years back.

MARY: You read it in the unaltered version?

LINCOLN: Well, I am both father and president,
  live in my declining years, and do not drink.

MARY: But what has happened to the Bible, sir?

LINCOLN: Oh, it's still published and well sold, I think.

MARY: It is Tad's time for bed.

LINCOLN: Good night, my son.

  (Exit Tad Lincoln)

MARY: You have left the Bible, Abe?

LINCOLN: No, Mary.

MARY: I haven't seen you read it of late.

LINCOLN: I haven't done so, is most likely why.
  But I haven't left it. I still own one.

MARY: Where is it, sir?

LINCOLN: It is tucked into bed
  where it belongs presently. It sleeps.

The Bible will wait my awakening
to it and perhaps come awake once more
itself to give meaning and direction
to the death of my dear Ann Hathaway,
a youthful love I cannot recover.
God took her and I do not fathom it.

MARY: By my life, it was not God who took her.

LINCOLN: But Mary, who else then if He exists?

MARY: Do Greek myths excel the Bible, Abe?

LINCOLN: I am not a literary critic;
    I venture no opinion, therefore.

MARY: How can I be hungry soon after dinner
    Mr. Lincoln?

LINCOLN: Are you hungry?

MARY: Famished.

LINCOLN: We all love you here, Mary Lincoln.

MARY: No, not all, not all. Mrs. Stanton
    has not been here so many long months.
    Why does Mrs. Stanton never visit
    anymore to the White House? Am I still
    First Lady?

LINCOLN: Yes, you are.

MARY: Well?

LINCOLN: Your hand, pet.

MARY: How judicious you are to ask my hand
    when I make a question. My hand you want.
    Are there no more answers for the first lady?

LINCOLN: Mary, I am forced to allocate time,
    some time at least, to our next election
    over Mr. McClellan who now runs up
    a tidy sum of money toward my seat.
    When I replaced him he then decided
    to replace me and will be his party's choice
    come election time.

MARY: What a general,
    here?

LINCOLN: Well, not here unless we cede it
    to him, but I need the time to figure
    a campaign. Please help me, I beg you.

MARY: I
    will help as best I can, Mr. Lincoln.
    I look forward to the people's choice
    with great anxiety.

LINCOLN: Do go upstairs,
    dear Mary.

MARY: Will we win?

LINCOLN: I suppose so.
  Will you look in on Tad as you go?

MARY: I will; I know my duty, Mr. Lincoln.

  (Exit Mary Lincoln)

SCENE 7

In the field. Longstreet's Corps. Dyer writing a letter, and soldiers.

DYER: Three whole major campaigns and not one word. I told her I'd fight for her and slavery and any damned thing else. But she's told me once she loved me and that's enough— In the very first letter. The only letter. It's been silence since. Still—I'll love her to the last blood in me. I will love General Lee and try my best to love General Longstreet, too.

ALFRED: Where we going now, Mother John?

JOHN: I don't know. I hear Gettysburg. They've got a new Union Commander, too.

ALFRED: So what? We got Lee, ain't we? We can go anywhere we want, I guess.

JOHN: He is a tough old man.

ALFRED: Tough is not the word, John. He can fight 'til hell freezes over and win a decision on the ice. He is too smart to beat. He'll take Washington before long. In fact, I suspect soon.

JOHN: We're headed there, alright. Say, Randy, where were you?

(Enter Randall)

RANDALL: Yonder.

JOHN: Where? Doing what?

RANDALL: I was bowling, Mother John, I was bowling.

JOHN: How do you bowl in an open field?

RANDALL: It's easy. You get yourself ten sticks from a tree and put 'em easy in the ground, then go get a cannon ball from someone in artillery and bowl.

ALFRED: Isn't that clever. He'll blow the whole regiment out of camp getting his exercise.

RANDALL: The whole regiment?

ALFRED: Whole thing.

RANDALL: Haw! Say, what d'you boys think about the rectum as a whole?

JOHN: That is a dirty crack, Randy, and not at all funny. *(The others laugh)*. The chaplain is nearby, and wouldn't it be awful if he heard you? There's no need for that kind of noise to fall on his ears; he is a good man. That goes for you too, Alfred.

RANDALL: I'm sorry, Mother John.

ALFRED: Johnnie, you're like a saint in hell. There's fire in your halo; wake up, man.

JOHN: Why don't we turn our jackets inside out and go serenade an officer, like we did yesterday?

RANDALL: A born singer! I'll bet you sing as soon as you're awake!

JOHN: I do not, and you know it; it's vulgar to be tuneful in the morning!

RANDALL: *(To Alfred)* Some songbird there alright. What are we doing here, anyway? I want after Yanks, I do.

ALFRED: Speaking of songbirds, I remember that field in front of us a week ago after the Yank's charge. I remember it at night with the white moon on it, their bodies, and the whippoorwill in the wood nearby. What would make a bird sing at midnight? It was terrible.

JOHN: I hope never again to see such carnage in the field. There were three Yanks not twenty feet from me at the wall who'd gotten musket balls in their faces, and, between the three, they couldn't have made a single wholesome set of features. I know, when we withdrew, they were still alive.

RANDALL: A dead Yank is a good Yank, Johnnie.

JOHN: A dead Yank is not a good Yank!

RANDALL: I say he is!

ALFRED: Randy, forget it. His brother serves under Grant.

RANDALL: Grant!

ALFRED: True, he's a Yank.

RANDALL: Good Lord, you'll never know what you have in your own ranks. I'm truly sorry, John; I hadn't known you'd had a divorce in the family.

JOHN: It's of no matter.

RANDALL: Now it's of no matter to him! Did you hear that?! No matter! I can't see what makes the lad move. Lice wouldn't take to him.

ALFRED: Let's have a game of baseball.

RANDALL: Well, who'll pitch?

ALFRED: I'll get up a team behind Crowther.

RANDALL: To heck with it. My boys won't play with him.

ALFRED: Oh, come on, now.

RANDALL: No, that's flat. He throws the ball too hard. Last game he came close to knocking the stuffing out of my boys. They won't play with him, I tell you.

ALFRED: That's plain poor sportsmanship of you, then.

RANDALL: Nossir, if I joined this army for any purpose at all, it was not to get killed playing baseball with that damn Crowther.

I'll pass, 'til you find a pitcher who ain't working for the Yankees.

ALFRED: You're a spoilsport, Randy.

RANDALL: Nope, I'm not. I've decided instead to try to talk my friend, Good John, here into liking me again because I never meant to make him look as glum as he is. I like him, and want him to like me. Good John? Mother John, fuss at me a little.

JOHN: *(Hums indifferently)*

RANDALL: Johnnie, don't sing in my face—that ain't polite. I really mean it when I say I'm sorry.

JOHN: (Hums)

RANDALL: I'm awful sorry.

JOHN: *(Hums)*

RANDALL: I'm terrible sorry

JOHN: *(Takes out a Bible exposing it plainly as a Bible, turns to a page well back and with an attitude of hurt self-righteousness, reads)*

RANDALL: You're right and I'm wrong, then. *(Silence)* I take it all back, anyway. A louse would love you, John. *(Silence)* And it's good to have you in this army. *(Short silence)* You're a terrific shot. *(Short silence)* Strike that last out if you don't care for it. *(Long silence)* I'm as sick of this war as you are and I wish it was over. How I wish it was over. My mother is agin' the whole idea, and didn't want to let me come at all. Now, that's unpatriotic, Johnnie. First thing she did when she knew I had thoughts on it was hide every gun belonging to us. *(Silence)* I don't even think Yank anymore; I'm shootin' squirrels. *(Short silence)* So I'm for stickin' together, John! *(Short silence), (Sings)* We are a band of brothers, and native to the soil—

JOHN: You are a double talker, Randy.

RANDALL: Anything, anything you want, but don't let me fritter away forlorn, Johnnie.

JOHN: You're not frittering away.

RANDALL: Well, I'm forlorn.

JOHN: Then you think you've had your medicine?

RANDALL: Yes, and it was good for me.

JOHN: You won't forget my feelings again?

RANDALL: I swear by General Lee.

JOHN: And by God?

RANDALL: Yeah, him too.

JOHN: Then we'll be friends.

RANDALL: *(Mopping his brow)* Whew, Mother John, you're as tough behind the lines as in 'em.

JOHN: And I think you have a flea or two. There's fleabane in that valley below.

RANDALL: I'll get some, I'll get some. And I itch to get on to Gettysburg, too.

JOHN: Say, we've passed mess time.

ALFRED: Again, I'm getting my goober peas.

(Goes to his haversack)

RANDALL: *(To Alfred)* You've whet my appetite.

JOHN: *(To Randall)* What have you got?

RANDALL: Hardtack.

JOHN: I can't eat it anymore.

RANDALL: Some Union rations?

JOHN: *(Whispering)* Get 'em, Randy. *(Randall goes to his haversack. Alfred has brought forth a chicken egg from his.)*

ALFRED: *(To the egg)* Oh, if I could have known your mother.

JOHN: Randy, look!

RANDALL: An egg!

JOHN: That it is, alright.

RANDALL: Damn.

JOHN: Damn.

RANDALL: Mother John!

JOHN: I couldn't help myself. I lust for that egg.

RANDALL: You've drooled down your shirt.

JOHN: It's true, spit over everything. That's a mean trick, Alfred. If you mean to eat it, you should have done it in private.

ALFRED: I don't think I'll eat it.

RANDALL: Are you tradin'?!

ALFRED: I think I am. *(John and Randall go for their possessions, preparing to barter.)*

RANDALL: I never saw you sneak off foraging.

ALFRED: Ah, well, what you don't see will never blind you, I say.

JOHN: All I've got is letters—some from my sister, a mess from my maw.

ALFRED: That's poor boot, John.

JOHN: I know.

RANDALL: Don't you worry, John, you want that egg?

JOHN: I want it so bad, I can't stop the spit coming.

RANDALL: Now, first, and this should do the trick, there's my pocket Bible, not a page missing, none torn.

ALFRED: Let me see. Aagh, printed in New York. Put it bye.

RANDALL: Will you add this ring to it? It was my father's. Solid silver, and worth proud money in better days.

ALFRED: No jewelry, thanks. I'm thinking of something to fit my stomach, not my finger.

RANDALL: Three biscuits.

ALFRED: Where did you get biscuits?

RANDALL: Never mind, I got 'em.

ALFRED: Three?

RANDALL: Four?

ALFRED: That's a start.

RANDALL: A strip of mule to go with it.

ALFRED: *(Feeling it)* Why, if you throw that against a wall, I believe it'd stick.

RANDALL: Yes or no?

ALFRED: With the biscuits, and keep coming on.

RANDALL: That's enough; you're puttin' the wood to me. I'm outta here for Gettysburg. Then Washington.

JOHN: I can taste that egg now, Randy.

RANDALL: A strip of sow belly. That's all I offer; I keep one for myself.

ALFRED: That sow belly has the tits on.

RANDALL: No extra charge.

ALFRED: Done, then. I'll swap for the biscuits, horsemeat and the pork. *(Takes it up)* Here's your egg, John. You have a good friend.

RANDALL: I hope he knows it.

JOHN: My first egg of the war.

ALFRED: I'll read you the last letter from my paw into the bargain. "Dear Son," he says. He either calls me son or boy. "I hear tell every week of troops going north from town and hope you are not among them. At least when I know you are in the South somewhere, you aren't too far from home, anyway. I got traded out of my best gun yesterday by a snake who had this egg that made my mouth water. It was the best looking pullet egg I've ever seen and I decided I had to have it. It was so big and felt so fresh that the man was a mile away at least before I saw it wasn't real. Some skunk had made it for just such purposes, swapping, that is. Even if it is an artful work, it is a devilish one, I think. So I am sending it to you to trade off to some Yank, for as much as you can get."

JOHN: Not real?

ALFRED: I never said it was.

RANDALL: Alfred, damn you, that's dirty bartering! *(John throws the egg away)* Hey! That's biscuits and meat you're throwing away. *(Retrieves the egg)* John, your mind is messed up, for sure. We can swap this egg for anything, wait and see. He traded low; we'll get more. If he's a maggot, we'll be worms.

JOHN: It's the principle of the thing that hurts.

RANDALL: Well, watch the principal I bring back with me. Before the war's over this egg will have been through every regiment in General Lee's army. I won't be long.

(Exit Randall, followed by John)

DYER: Signed: Your loving Tom. That finishes it. Now, lets get on to this Gettysburg.

SCENE 8

The field. Lees camp. Lee, Taylor. Intense battle sound.

LEE: You say Pickett's men are now engaged, Colonel?

TAYLOR: As you wished, sir.

LEE: They will take Meade apart.
    Don't fret so, you have a hangdog look.

TAYLOR: Sir, a messenger is coming fast.

LEE: He has ridden his horse near death, the fool.

(Enter messenger)

MESSENGER: *(Proffering the message. He is stone faced.)*

LEE: Pickett is destroyed, our best hopes shackled.
    This is all my fault and I will own to it
    the rest of my days. I have failed our nation,
    I have failed these excellent armies.
    Come, Sir, we must get our men out of war
    and into safety. God has not seen fit
    to favor us or spare humiliation.
    I pray my tears may not prevent these eyes
    from finding safe retreat. Come, Colonel.

SCENE 9

Sound of moving troops. Randall and John. Drums.

RANDALL: Thank heaven for a chance to rest, John.

JOHN: How d'you feel, Randy?

RANDALL: Terrible. My head is broke, I'm sure of it. I will never make it back to Richmond.

JOHN: Yes, you will.

RANDALL: I won't, and know it. I'm sick to death of fightin' an' just want to die off. Never could stomach again what I saw here, anyway. I've had it all, John, had every lick this war or any other could ever show me. I am a dying dog.

JOHN: I won't hear you talk like that.

RANDALL: Just catch me when I fall, Mother John.

JOHN: I'll see you home.

RANDALL: Did you see that fellow die on his feet this morning? I didn't know we carried our own grave markers. Lord, it seems an army is a well prepared thing, when you think of it.

JOHN: Woe is me; what'll befall us now?

RANDALL: I won't live to know; I hope there's victory for us yet.

50

JOHN: How can it be? We're whipped bad this time. This army really hurts, Randy. There's dead and grieving everywhere. We are smashed up is what.

RANDALL: My head hurts something awful.

JOHN: I can't wrap that bandage right. Here. *(Re-wraps Randall's bandage)* It's a nasty smack, alright. Hold still. You have always been a good friend to me, Randy. Remember Alfred, the rascal, cheating you out of your goods with that egg? You did that for me; I wanted that egg. Then you went and really swapped it off on someone good. I wonder where that egg is now.

RANDALL: I remember it, alright. I remember the beating Alfred gave to that Dyer boy, too, for writing silly love letters.

JOHN: But he set it right, too. When he saw Dyer hit by that shell he stopped to pull him up behind a tree, and they both got it, then, from a Yank rifleman. I really thought much of Dyer, I guess.

RANDALL: He was game as hell, and I liked him, too.

JOHN: *(Finished wrapping)* There. That'll get you home.

RANDALL: Not me, not me.

JOHN: Are you alright?

RANDALL: No, I'm not. Oh, no, I'm not.

JOHN: Is it your head?

RANDALL: Look. I've got a nose bleed.

JOHN: You're hemorrhaging!

RANDALL: That's bad, isn't it?

JOHN: Lie down, Randy, be quiet. I'll get a medic.

RANDALL: Don't you leave me.

JOHN: Oh, my God, don't you leave me! Be still.

RANDALL: Shortly, not now. You know who has the egg?

JOHN: I don't have a care in the world for that.

RANDALL: Well, I know. It's P.F.C. Albert Durham in the Second Company an' he'll give it back to you for the askin'. He's a good boy. You get that egg.

JOHN: Randy——!

RANDALL: You get it, hear?

JOHN: I will. *(Silence)*

RANDALL: 'Bye, Mother John. *(Dies)*

JOHN: Oh, Lord, you take the best*! (Weeps quietly over Randall's body)* We are broken men. Broken men. *(Weeps)* All of the best.

(Weeps) Randy, Randy. What to do now?

(Enter Lee)

JOHN: Oh, Sir, heaven bless you, General Lee. I wish he could
see you here. It would have been a moment of greatness for him,
as well as me.

LEE: I think it would kill my God to look on me;
he was lucky to escape my sight.
Now there is need to command your army;
the man you cradle there, what was his name?

JOHN: Randall Taylor, sir.

LEE: I once knew a man named Carpenter.
To be a Taylor, Carpenter, or Smith
at war, is to need an abode of Lee.
Is there a Thomas Dyer in your ranks?

JOHN: Yessir.

LEE: Where is Mr. Dyer now, please tell me.

JOHN: Being pure at heart as he was, sir—

LEE: I do understand you.

JOHN: Yes sir, a shell, took his whole side away. Alfred Moss tried
to save his remains but a Yank skirmisher drove lead into both

of them.

LEE: When you're ready,
then, help me get this army on the road.

(Drums)

Scene 10

Washington. The White House. Lincoln, Seward, and Stanton.

(Enter Stanton)

STANTON: Lincoln, you are fast dying, I believe,
    for news like this, so I'll give it straight 'way;
    Vicksburg's ours and Gettysburg is won,
    all in a day. Shall I read it again, sir?

SEWARD: Did you hear it, Mr. President?

LINCOLN: I'm not sure; would you read it again, Stanton?

STANTON: Vicksburg is ours and Gettysburg's won.
    Pemberton's army of thirty thousand
    has given in to Grant and Meade has scored
    against Lee, driving him off to Virginia.

LINCOLN: Driving him off? Can't he capture that man?

STANTON: Nossir, but has forced a full retreat.

LINCOLN: I will have a heart attack if this is false.

STANTON: Sir, I hope I know by now when to wait,
    and when to pronounce.

LINCOLN: You hear the same, Seward?

SEWARD: I wouldn't hear anything else for the world.

LINCOLN: This is the best I have felt in two years
    of anxious waiting and hopeful replacing
    of one officer after another.
    It is such great news I cannot weigh it
    in meaning's scale. It so lightens the brain.
    It is a meadowlark's song, Stanton;
    you cannot have sung it at all, I think.
    It has a pure ascending note, I must
    by all means learn by rote and return
    in singing to you: We've won, Stanton.

STANTON: Now you've got me, sir. I'll go raise the press.

(Exit Stanton)

LINCOLN: Seward, we've won.

SEWARD: Lincoln, you've got a tear.

LINCOLN: Damned if I don't. Does it become me?

(Enter Mary)

MARY: Yours are for happiness, mine for losses
    too much to lift alone. Come help me, Abe.
    My Kentucky kin are dying at a rate
    past bearing. Help, oh, help an oppressed wife
    up and away from despair. We have doves
    who sing of their excesses, do we not?
    May we? Mais, oui. But I am obliged not.

Our battlefields paint themselves in clover.
It was my dear brother last year who fell
and I, too, fell prey to a divided joy
for a Union victory and remorse
for a brother's loss in that same engagement!
What am I to do, Abe? Elate or break?!
I try to be faithful to too many!
But should I not feel loss for a brother
since he is my deadly enemy? Help,
sir, if you will. I require some support
and definition in this grisly matter.
Now I hear of a win at Gettysburg
and the loss of my dearest sister's husband
there. How shall I respond? Shall I curtsy?
Cut off my hair? Wear mourning robes of black
or victory's ribbons? Tell me, sir, tell me;
I need an answer. I'm not doing well.

LINCOLN: My dear Mary, I had offered him rank
as major in our Union forces
but he chose secession. I could do no more.
Still I grieve his loss as you do now
and will have a letter sent his wife
to join us here at the White House promptly.

SEWARD: On my word, a rebel's wife here, sir?

LINCOLN: If you have never known a good enemy,
Seward, you will shortly.

SEWARD: And I learn fast.

MARY: I would like to celebrate Gettysburg
    with you, but convictions aside, cannot.
    Somehow Emily is more important
    than mere real estate and I thank you
    for thinking she will come, but I do not.

LINCOLN: I will draft the letter myself.

MARY: Oh, will
    you, now. May I not write my own sister?

LINCOLN: As you wish.

MARY: Oh, Abe, now I turn and point
    my own husband, you I love. Forgive me.
    I am shifting plates below the earth's crust
    trying not to crack her still composure.
    Tell me how to keep happiness within,
    somehow to soften the malcontent
    and merciless movement of inhuman war.
    How insulate oneself. How do you, sir?

LINCOLN: I try but fail, there is an undertow
    to the best of currents that drowns the spirit
    as it would regale itself in success.
    There is no pleasure in succeeding;
    one posts and fences against intrusion,
    is all, and hopes the post holes are dug deep.

MARY: Mine, I suppose, then, are shallow and weak.

LINCOLN: Women are closest to peacetime powder,
    men to war's, it seems, and where we enjoy
    the effects of yours, ours bring misery
    to you, and I cannot for my quick life
    ponder why this should be but to presume
    one more argument for nature's devil,
    imbalance—that character of living
    that affords one tree more growth than another.

SEWARD: While our arts pursue balance.

LINCOLN: They must, Seward,
    in order to be greater than the thing
    portrayed. Ordering people's attentions
    to witness disorder is no mean task,
    making a workman in charge of his tools.

MARY: Oh, Abe, spare me your opinions on art
    and nature while I grieve. I am open
    as an unhealed wound to everything in
    or out of balance, to things speakable
    or not, understandable or dumb.
    Torn flesh, sir, for the loss of sons and brothers
    hardly leaves me fresh for apt discussions
    of art and matter.

LINCOLN: My apology.

SEWARD: And mine, Mrs. Lincoln.

MARY: And I should try,
    I guess, to fathom the complexity,

the prismatic wonders, of the male mind
that can transcend such trivial matters
of life and death as it happens to one
member of our kind at a time and bring
to focus the great reach of your concern
for the competitiveness of your armies—
both theirs and ours. But I see you
avoid my point by dealing in numbers.
My way concentrates, yours is distributive.
Mine costs, yours pays dividends. Whatever
I say now must not be held against me.
I am resolute in argument,
Mr. Seward, as the President
will confess without prompting, whether or not
I am correct, d'you hear? Whether or not.

SEWARD: I hear, Madam.

MARY: Mine costs, yours pay dividends.
    You comprehend my meaning, do you not?

LINCOLN: Mary,—

MARY: There, you see? I can't have my grief
    but Mr. Lincoln closes his court
    on me and I am left to rag and blossom
    when I may, to all purposes alone
    and out of hearing by our most exalted
    leadership. They are hard at work at their math.
    And the meadowsweet are all crushed under.

LINCOLN: Mary, we will honor your grief and note
   our differences.

MARY: And let there be peace.

LINCOLN: Peace.

(Exit Mary)

          My regrets for the incident.

SEWARD: A cultured lady stressed to the hilt, Sir.

LINCOLN: Thank you, Seward. She has had it hard.

SEWARD: She has, indeed, yet you show greater wear
   at the cuffs, your gait erodes to plain plodding
   and speech goes slack waiting for the mind
   to bloom even out of its season.

LINCOLN: Yes, war is not the proper season for it,
   Seward. My mind seems slower now to me.

SEWARD: Of course, wear and tear. The inky stallion
   you fear riding before the war's finish
   concerns you, no, not concerns but weighs on you
   too much. Disavow death, make it exempt
   from your thought. Kiss it off entirely.

LINCOLN: Like getting rid of my body's trunk, man.
   I can't unsheath that thinking without my
   finding I have put a bare blade in hand.

Death is an all-time preoccupation
I have made room for in every pocket.
Do I have a musty odor, Seward?

SEWARD: Nothing like, Sir.

LINCOLN: Now my secretary
   carefully extrudes by formulation
   all letters of threat to me or family
   so we can't know how many times we die
   by acclamation. I would rather know,
   you know, so that I might on occasion
   find fault in syntax, bloated metaphor
   or a spelling denoting ignorance
   of a kind but, no, it's all out of sight
   by thoughtless secretarial decree.
   I am eager to know we'll win this game
   and that I may rule a United States
   olive branched, soothed and united once more.
   Oh, I must reach that heavenly plateau,
   Dear Seward, it is the only reward
   I seek.

SEWARD: What would you like done, sir? Name it.

LINCOLN: We will re-hang the sun so low in the sky
   that the length of shadow will darken
   the Southern issue of slavery. Gone,
   the lingering malice of vulgar war
   will have to find some other vocal line
   for its vile and wasteful continuance.
   Slavery will no more be an issue.

Then we will pursue this peevish conflict
'til their bones snap, and opposition
is an article for casual dismay.

SEWARD: Good heaven, where will it all end, Lincoln?

LINCOLN: Well, Seward, let's give thanks for Gettysburg.
    I have spent two years waiting for this day.
    Two years waited is as many wasted.
    And two from the four-year term of office
    leaves me half the time for twice the work
    my post would normally require. Hurry,
    time beckons to us. We must consume her.
    The rebels at last have been soundly hurt
    and will employ the hours we accord them
    to lick their wounds. We must not play infirmary
    to them. Come. God, I am like a wild boar
    that, tearing its adversary tastes blood,
    raises the fur along its supple spine
    and stands off scuffing the ground, leveling
    a hateful eye on his grounded victim.
    One meaning, and one alone, I have now
    to charge, fracture, and eviscerate,
    disjoint and disembowel, show no mercy,
    give no time to collect the fallen dead,
    but pace a war so destructively
    that wisdom in it has no good place,
    decision no direction. So to that
    we will give our next eye and energy,
    for rebellion was loudly warned against,
    Seward, all routes of mediation opened
    to them and all approaches honored.

They took the foolish course of damned war,
in this our anger is most justified.
Let us go plan thanks to Meade for victory
midway in this affair and move about
the second half of conflict. Then I'll turn
my attention to election over
McClellan who is coming on fast.

SEWARD: Is he anywhere near us, do you think?

LINCOLN: I have beat him out of the paddock by
being here first. He will pay good money
to lose, I think.

SCENE 11

A room in the White House. Lincoln alone at a desk.

(Enter Emilie Helm)

EMILIE: I hardly meant to interrupt you, Sir,
    I lost my way in the White House hallways.

LINCOLN: Oh, Emilie, it's a joy to see you.
    We have losses to share, yours a husband,
    mine a son, yours from one side a contest,
    mine another. At one and the same time
    man attacks his kind and would console it.
    We have much to learn of our angry shape.
    Thank you for responding to my letter
    and letting Mary share our home with you.
    Welcome, welcome and do sit down with me.

EMILIE: I, of course, miss my husband, as a light
    in the firmament is gone to the eye
    of one who studies firmaments, you know.

LINCOLN: I know it well. Flesh is disposable
    both in single units most meaningfully
    and in the thousands, less understood.
    But being here with your sister, Mary,
    is some condolence, I hope.

EMILIE: It is, Sir,
    And I hope to her, as well.

LINCOLN: I'm sure.
   She needs you, as apple its nurturing tree.

EMILIE: As grape, it's vine.

LINCOLN: No less, Emilie, no less.
   She was disconsolate without you.

EMILIE: Always the family bulwark, the starched one,
    she constructed lives for us to live,
    made projections that wisdom might follow
    and saw to it that God knew our places.

LINCOLN: And did He?

EMILIE: When she was done, he hardly
   knew his own, I think.

LINCOLN: She drove me to this
   office as though she commanded the horse
   that carried me. She wanted a president
   for a husband and got it. Now all apart
   for what comes next, she wanders the hallways,
   though loss of something to do and someone
   to do it with may be some similar,
   I do not know.

EMILIE: I do, oh yes, I do.
   Suffering both together, I do know.
   My man is interred with the grubs and worms
   and cannot steer me anymore this way
   or that and therefore lacking not only him,

I search the woods for purpose. It is numbing.
You're winning the war over us at last,
now, and still must gain your reelection.
Your life is all contest, Sir.

LINCOLN:　　　　　　　　　It is that.

EMILIE: And mid-war, too.

LINCOLN:　　　　　　　　　Nothing halts elections,
　　Emilie. No war, pestilence, famine
　　or holocaust must interrupt the need
　　for people to change their minds at midday
　　and deny their trust, much as our Union
　　feels your confederated southern states
　　threw off the cloak of Union for a new shirt.

EMILIE: You are in two wars at once.

LINCOLN:　　　　　　　　　　I suppose.

EMILIE: With my sister, Mary, not quite herself,
　　that's three.

LINCOLN: If you don't stop adding, I'll quit
　　before the larger numbers bury me.

EMILIE: You are not known as a quitter down south, Sir.

LINCOLN: Oh, Emilie, war was immanent,
　　I know, but was my supply of that fort
　　at Charleston a cause for such bloodshed?

EMILIE: The issue unresolved would have brought war
    sooner or later and our Beauregard
    firing on the fort hardly helped matters.
    Supplying the fort was neither helpful
    nor cause, I trust.

LINCOLN: I can thank you for that
    and do.

EMILIE: Then you're in my debt, I think.

LINCOLN: I am, and pay my debts responsibly,
    I believe.

EMILIE: Oh, do you? Do you always?

LINCOLN: A matter of discipline to do so.

EMILIE: May I take that as a Lincolnian
    verity, a pledge as well as statement?

LINCOLN: Emilie, by law you're my sister
    and need not secure promises from me.
    What I express to you I stand beside
    as I would for any family member.

EMILIE: Then may I make a bold request?

LINCOLN: You may.

EMILIE: My dead husband, Ben, whom you so kindly

offered rank to come north but who ended
south a general, waived your rich paychecks
for an unsteady currency and love
of his homeland. So life was difficult,
in simplest terms, for some diseased time.
He sold our home, our horses, and our livestock
but the money he took in was worthless.
It shriveled in the hand and decomposed.

LINCOLN: I've seen our worthwhile Union cash do that.

EMILIE: The difference between air and matter, Sir.

LINCOLN: Agreed, then.

EMILIE: Between something and nothing.
    Selling was discarding, then, and storage
    came next to hedge the time and hope for calm.
    No calm has come, only need has. I think
    I am going to allow myself a tear.

LINCOLN: Take what you need of those, dear Emilie.

EMILIE: I will and I thank you for your kindness.

LINCOLN: Born of need and privy to disaster.

EMILIE: Some security was found in storage
    but when Ben died the sun withdrew itself
    and dark need stalked the day. It was my need
    that he had planned for and it leapt to life.
    The money I had was Confederate,

useless. Home gone, I rushed to find my place
in the world or anywhere. The storage,
as it turned out, was larger than I dreamt.
He had squirreled six hundred bales of cotton
for us that I would now need to exist.
To sell it in the South, unthinkable,
though in the North a real price is ready.
The goods must be permitted for travel
by you and I ask you let them come north.
For your sister-by-law.

LINCOLN: My great regard
    for your husband's thoughtful disposition
    of resources. It's plain that he loved you.
    I had always admired his conduct
    toward you. It was gentle, questioning, kind.

EMILIE: He was your brother-in-law.

LINCOLN: Yes, brother.

EMILIE: May I hope your great regard rewards him?

LINCOLN: I had always regarded him that way,
    Emilie, he had great strength of purpose,
    a lion's saunter carried it, I thought.
    I will not fail to regard a brother
    but caution you, the sale of cotton
    in the North is a heady, even perilous
    pursuit. You would need an agent, surely.

EMILIE: Agents take fat fees and stout commissions.

LINCOLN: I am troubled here, I must confess it.

EMILIE: I see that.

LINCOLN: There is quite a danger here;
   cotton could be taken as contraband.

EMILIE: I reasoned I had you in my debt, Sir,
   and would see you pay your debt responsibly.

LINCOLN: I remember.

EMILIE: Matter of discipline,
   you said.

LINCOLN: You could have been a lawyer.
   I see you have been at work on me.

EMILIE: You designated me your sister, Abe.

LINCOLN: And sisters will do that to their brothers?

EMILIE: That cotton is my survival!

LINCOLN: For now,
   perhaps, but I would rather care for you
   myself than turn over that rebel crop
   for sale in a country at war with you,
   wherein profit goes to an enemy.

EMILIE: We are enemies?

LINCOLN: No, our countries are
   and we are bound to them with fealty
   and duty. There is an answer to this
   but not one to your liking, Emilie.
   An oath of allegiance to my Union
   allows me freedom from the title traitor
   and secures your permit.

EMILIE: Oath to Union?!

LINCOLN: Preserves you from unjust complicity
   charges and perhaps one of treason, too.

EMILIE: My husband dead by your hand and I pledge
   allegiance to your dumb, prosaic flag?
   Am I such a contradictory fool?
   I am dedicated to my husband
   and to his dedication! Nothing else!

LINCOLN: Then let me set you an annuity.

EMILIE: Buy me off my purpose, Mr. Lincoln?

LINCOLN: My dear Emilie—

EMILIE: Secure promises
   from you I needn't do, you say.

LINCOLN: Sorry,
   but I think you led me there, attorney.

EMILIE: Profane my husband's name is what you ask.

LINCOLN: No, now, and you have enlarged your treatise.

EMILIE: Yes, and enter my soul into slavery
to you the rest of my miserable days.
White slavery! Despicable brother!

LINCOLN: I hardly think I earned that, Emilie.

EMILIE: No, nor do I. I leapt to defend.
I promise to leave the White House tomorrow.

LINCOLN: Unnecessary, but as you wish.

(Exit Lincoln)

EMILIE: I
do wish

(Enter Mary opposite)

MARY: Tad was having his nap, but where is Abe?
Oh, Emilie, what is the matter?

EMILIE: I
am going to my room to pack.

MARY: For where,
pack? Where is there to go with war on?

EMILIE: South, where I belong and you, too, Mary.

MARY: Me?

EMILIE: Four of your five brothers are Confederates,
    three of your four sisters married officers
    there. Why try to find yourself in this house?
    Come with me. Make a family united
    and be among those who love and cherish you.
    We could leave together.

MARY: Are you quite mad?

EMILIE: Yes, I believe I am. I'll not trouble
    you further.

MARY: But Emilie!

EMILIE: No more please!

MARY: Are you leaving?

EMILIE: No, Mary I am gone!

    (Exit Emilie)

SCENE 12

Scene is the White House. Present are Stanton, Seward, others.

STANTON: Seward, there's a saint in every window,
idol in each heart, of every Northerner
in these states. There's a stein in every hand,
and mayhem between the bedposts, of all
our voters. There's intelligence in the world,
after all.

SEWARD: Hardly expected as it is.

STANTON: Always look for the unexpected.

SEWARD: I do, but it's usually against me,
not for. Why should replacement finger us?
I have served Lincoln well and so have you.

STANTON: Why, it's enough that Mrs. Stanton
fails to visit Mary at the White House
to have me cashiered. Any reason's
reason enough. You have a mole, Seward.

SEWARD: Well, Holy Moley! So what? You've seen it.

STANTON: It's reason. Lincoln's mole is imposed on,
don't you see? You strike his originality.
His reelection gives him a choice
of one whole new cabinet, if he pleases.

Risks of the game, trademark of servants.
I'll open a dry-goods store. What will you do?

SEWARD: Oh, Stanton, please. Your humor fades me.

STANTON: It's true, you do look faded, but you must plan.

SEWARD: If I'm released, I'll transport myself south
and run against Jeff Davis for President.
They're in need down there.

STANTON: I'll be your white slave.
You must not abuse a time of nonsense,
sir, by being sensible in it. Why,
what if our Southern states had used their senses
lately? We would have no war. No war
contracts your fame and ushers you out
of immortality as easily
as conflict could escort you in. I swear,
don't knock our nonsense, it has put us here.

SEWARD: I hope it, or something, will keep us here.

STANTON: Nonsense will, if all else fails, I trust.
The fact remains, Lincoln has won reelection
and I'm happy for him. Here he comes.

SEWARD: I don't hear anything.

STANTON: I heard his voice.
Confound. Discussed in any other terms
than the most flattering and sympathetic

he explodes in past servants, dogs, cats,
latched doors, thrown bolts and armed guards even.
But let your words be candied for a week
and he'll be seen nowhere in Washington.
I swear, if he were not our President
I'd take him for a sleuth from the police.

SEWARD: I know what you mean—

STANTON: —Or a watchdog.
    No one wins who plays!

(Enter Lincoln)

LINCOLN: Plays what, Stanton?

STANTON: It doesn't matter, Sir; there's no winning.

LINCOLN: Well, I disagree, we have just won new terms
    for ourselves.

STANTON: That was no play.

LINCOLN: When you win,
    you may call it what you like, the choice is yours.
    It's the loser who can find no words for it.

STANTON: A toast to that, if I understand you.

(Seward and Stanton pour drinks)

LINCOLN: It is human nature, I suppose, that
    they should choose one man to hang success on,
    but how unfair. My entire cabinet
    is sleepless with the warlong drudgery,
    our generals worn out with kept pursuit.
    I am simply symbol of that labor,
    you are its signature. Good cabinet
    men are rare and once discovered should be kept.
    I hope you have plans in that same direction
    since I have no mind to disown your loyalty
    or let you take rest. Our nation needs you.
    I need you, and I beg you to stay.

SEWARD: Do you know you are the first president
    of northern origin twice in office?

LINCOLN: Well, so I am. I'll finish drinking to that.

BOTH: To Lincoln! *(A knock at the door. Stanton attends it, returns
    with a dispatch).*

STANTON: May I read it, Mr. President? *(Lincoln nods)*
    "Congratulations on your victory. My men were so overwhelmed
    with joy that they promptly took Atlanta for you. May you reign
    in good health. Obediently yours, General W.T. Sherman."

SEWARD: Lincoln, it's ours, the Southern storehouse!

STANTON: Well, now, messages are at my office,
    surely. I'll have a full day's work there.

When generals win colossal objectives,
requisitions fly in like locusts.

SEWARD: You must have a hall full of petitioners
by now and I'm due at the Capitol.
My warm regards to Sherman.

STANTON: And mine, sir.

LINCOLN: Good day, both of you. I'll convey your thoughts.
It has been a most propitious day.

*(Exit Seward, Stanton, Lincoln showing them to the door. He signals
out the door, presumably to someone responsible for the petitioners)*

Let them come in.

*(Enter the petitioners. There is one quite madly dressed woman, a
gentle woman and a young man appearing nervous and impatient.
Lincoln seats himself behind a desk. Each petitioner stands opposite
the desk)*

LINCOLN: Well, then, who first?

WOMAN: Mr. President, your Honor, will you give me a position
in one of your hospitals? I can do the work of a doctor but will
settle for position as a nurse. I am a clairvoyant.

LINCOLN: Indeed.

WOMAN: Yes, Mr. President. These eyes of mine see all—all. Through things, through people, even, oh, yes, through ideas. See all. I can see right into your heart this very minute, your lungs, your liver, and what do you think I see with my spirit eyes? Eh, what do you think I see?

LINCOLN: Why, for one thing, quite enough, Madam.

WOMAN: Oh, yes, enough but more. Of course you don't know. It isn't given to you to know. Suffering does it, suffering gives it to you. I want to work in a hospital to help our men raise themselves. Do you think you might have a place for me?

LINCOLN: Well, no, I think not. You know rather too much for a hospital.

WOMAN: I have had a vision, Sir, being a thing of God as I am. You are a religious man, aren't you? I would heal and teach God to those in the hospitals.

LINCOLN: I tell you confidentially, woman, and you must not breathe a word of this, those fellows at the hospitals are a rough lot. Religion's not to be rubbed into them by anyone weighing less than two hundred pounds and not carrying a cudgel. And, of course, if they have no faith, you can do them no good.

WOMAN: That's true, Sir; if they have no faith, I cannot help them.

LINCOLN: There you are, then. Be at peace, and go home.

WOMAN: I am too sensitive, perhaps I'd not survive the hospitals. Best go home, best to go home. Thank you Sir, your Honor, thank you. *(Produces a prodigious hand for Lincoln to take, and–)*

(Exit woman)

YOUNG MAN: *(Coming forward)* These are my credentials, Mr. President. *(Flocks of papers)* You'll see they're all in order.

LINCOLN: Sir, it would take me all day to read those. Just tell me your purpose.

YOUNG MAN: There is a vacancy under the Postmaster-General that I would like and these letters prove I am able and honest.

LINCOLN: Why, the papers prove nothing; they merely make statements. Proof is in performance.

YOUNG MAN: Try me, Sir, and you'll find me ambitious and trustworthy. If you would just read a few of these.

LINCOLN: Those make a veritable library. I'll pass on them, but I do believe the Postmaster-General should appoint his own vacancies.

YOUNG MAN: I came to you, Sir.

LINCOLN: Well, you came to the wrong place. There are twenty men courting that position. If I were to pick the man for it, I would acquire nineteen enemies. I have enough of those already. Please apply to the Postmaster-General. If you're capable, he'll have you, I'm sure.

YOUNG MAN: But, sir,—

LINCOLN: What else can I do for you?

YOUNG MAN: Is that all?

LINCOLN: I presume so. Who is next?

(Exit the young man)

LINCOLN: Mrs. Harvey, is it?

MRS. HARVEY: You are tired of seeing me, I suppose.

LINCOLN: *(Indicates her to sit.)* Mrs. Harvey, this is your sixth visit in as many days. When you are finished with me, I will see you in my dreams. It matters little whether we confront now or then because I am resigned to seeing you at one time or the other.

MRS. HARVEY: I regret, Sir, to add a feather's weight to the burden you already carry. But my visit to the south convinces me that Southern climates are no place for Northern soldiers to convalesce. It is too hot. I myself became ill in Mississippi. Sir, I have seen Northern men dying of fever and heat in St. Louis who might readily recuperate further north.

LINCOLN: I am sick of this subject of Northern hospitals.

MRS. HARVEY: If you will permit sick men to come north, you will improve the number that return to ranks ten to one.

LINCOLN: If your reasoning were correct, your argument would be a good one. I don't see how sending one sick man north will give us ten of good health.

MRS. HARVEY: You understand me, I think.

LINCOLN: Yes, yes, I do. But they will desert in route.

MRS. HARVEY: I don't think so. I believe in them and that's why I'm here.

LINCOLN: Believe away, Madam. Do you know how many deserters we have daily?

MRS. HARVEY: No, sir.

LINCOLN: The number would appall you.

MRS. HARVEY: Do they number more than those remaining?

LINCOLN: No, of course not.

MRS. HARVEY: Then they are the exception, not the rule. I believe in the rank of our men, not those exceptions.

LINCOLN: The exceptions are too many.

MRS. HARVEY: With all respects, Sir, just as you govern in the
name of the majority, so do I entreat in the same.

LINCOLN: This is your opinion.

MRS. HARVEY: Nossir, it's yours. You said desertions were fewer
than the loyalties. But I would rather have stayed at home than
come here and used your own admissions against you.

LINCOLN: *(Smiling)* I wish you had.

MRS. HARVEY: I can see you are tired. But I know that men will
die if I lose this petition. And if you accept it, you will be glad
for the rest of your life, I promise it.

LINCOLN: I was glad once, Mrs. Harvey, but I shall never be glad
anymore.

MRS. HARVEY: Oh, do not say so, Mr. Lincoln. This war will
finish someday.

LINCOLN: I know, I know, but so will I.

MRS. HARVEY: Do you sleep well nights, sir?

LINCOLN: No, I was never good at sleeping, and it gets worse as
time runs.

MRS. HARVEY: *(Standing)* Mr. Lincoln, I will let you back to your
business. I have taken too much of your time again.

LINCOLN: And then what?

MRS. HARVEY: I will come tomorrow.

LINCOLN: Dear Lady, sit down. *(She does)* Do you never tire?

MRS. HARVEY: Not so long as men die, sir. Not so long as there is life in me to spare life and not so long as there is life in me to give life.

LINCOLN: In a word, you are wholly devoted to the coming and going of mankind. You are exceedingly kind and generous, a credit to our country and a gift to womanhood. This evening I will draft an order for the first such hospital and specify it be erected in your state. You may procure a copy of the order in the morning at Mr. Stanton's office. Did you hear me? Did you hear me?

MRS. HARVEY: God bless you, oh, God bless you, sir.

LINCOLN: Will that suffice?

MRS. HARVEY: You have been very kind, and I am grateful for it. May I return once more tomorrow, for a moment, to thank you again?

LINCOLN: I would be happy to see you.

MRS. HARVEY: Thank you, Sir. Please excuse me, I am all apart for the moment.

LINCOLN: Mrs. Harvey, tell me, what would you have done if I'd
  said no.

MRS. HARVEY: I would have been outside that door at nine
  o'clock tomorrow morning.

LINCOLN: Then I have acted wisely.

MRS. HARVEY: God bless you, Abraham Lincoln.

  (Exit Mrs. Harvey)

SCENE 13

The Wilderness, an area south of the Rapidan River, of woods, marshes, swamps, and jungle. Grant and Colonel Rawlins, his adjutant-general and friend. Sound of marching troops outside. Background, war.

RAWLINS: Lee withdraws into the wilderness, Grant,
    where numbers mean nothing, every tree
    is obstacle to us and shield to him.
    Do we follow?

GRANT: If Mister Lee withdraws
    to the latrine, Rawlins, we must follow.

(Enter General Meade)

GRANT: Well, General Meade, it's good to see you.

MEADE: General Grant, Colonel Rawlins, thank you.
    I have two brigades confronting Lee.
    I believe it's Lee.

GRANT: Who else would it be, Sir?

MEADE: Grant, there's no telling. The woods are so thick
    that ricochet's a living danger
    to the man who dares unload his firepiece.
    A man in one of Hancock's companies
    smashed his rifle against the trunk of an oak,
    swearing it was safer to fight hand combat.

GRANT: I have already heard about the trees.

RAWLINS: Shall I have
    Burnside cover Meade's men, Sir?

GRANT: Yes, if you please, John.

(Exit Rawlins)

Well, we are dangerously underway.

MEADE: I admire your western victories;
    your generalship is firm and tight,
    but pray don't underestimate him:
    he is every muscle a ready soldier
    and every turn of mind the furtive fox.

GRANT: Did you beat him once or do I dream that?

MEADE: He erred in his judgement, that's so, I guess.

GRANT: I'd lay odds he even sleeps and eats
    as we do, harnesses as good a horse
    as any orderly, dies of stiffness
    from too much saddle and catches a cold
    unless bundled against inclement weather.
    He and I had service in the same war
    as lesser officers, in Mexico,
    that churly and despicable affront
    against a small foe that gathered Texas
    to our boundaries and stained our history.

MEADE: I neither have your anger nor your will
    but am pledged to ending this slaughter
    as you are. Keep peace within you, Grant,
    and I will keep my command alert
    to your quickest order. Now, I am needed
    at my front.

GRANT: Touch Lee, but don't engage, Meade.
    Just touch him for now. And send in Rawlins,
    if you will.

MEADE: Right, Sir.

(Exit Meade, enter Rawlins)

RAWLINS: Touch? Did you say touch Lee?
    Meade's amused.

GRANT: Yes, I think I said that.

RAWLINS: Well, it's got the old man all atwitter.
    He says no one lays a glove on Lee,
    but what a slap is returned and that's engagement,
    call it what you will.

GRANT: Well, if he's amused,
    good, How am I doing, John?

RAWLINS: Splendid, Sam.

GRANT: I hold rein over three hundred thousand,
    history's largest force.

RAWLINS: You're colorful, Sam,
    winning victories and drinking spirits.
    Inhuman in battle and too human out.

GRANT: I drink to life's grand insanity
    and would drink more if friends prevented me less.

RAWLINS: Well, those friends, too, are why you're here, you
    know. You have victory, drink, and friendship.
    What man could ask more?

GRANT: Could I ask a wee one?

RAWLINS: Ask, yes. Get, no.   .

GRANT: Well, I asked.

RAWLINS: And I heard.

GRANT: But you heard me request it.

RAWLINS: A wee thought.

GRANT: But don't I rank here?

RAWLINS: And a rank thought.

GRANT: It is just like at home. Dear Mrs. Grant

puts it under lock and key and adds surveillance.
Anything else I am in command of,
but not that hickory cabinet. Did you hide it?

RAWLINS: I poured it in the Rapidan this morning.

GRANT: Oh, you are a brute, John—my good whiskey
in the river! Good grief, man, it will run
downstream into the damned rebel camp!

RAWLINS: You'll do without it.

GRANT: Oh, I've no doubt,
it was good Jack Daniels, I hope you know.

RAWLINS: *(Mocking)* No.

GRANT: Yes.

RAWLINS: Is that good?

GRANT: Is that good!

RAWLINS: I see.

GRANT: Savage, pure savage. Well, I want to find
our quartermaster corps—let's go.

RAWLINS: With you.

(Exit Grant and Rawlins)

SCENE 14

Scene is Cold Harbor. Lee and Taylor, his adjutant. Night. Enter Taylor. Occasional musketry.

TAYLOR: General Lee, it does no good to win.
　　The Federal army is too large and strong.
　　We have traded them huge casualties
　　now in three places, they do not lay back.

LEE: Well, would you call that winning the field?

TAYLOR: Nossir. But we've not lost, either, have we?

LEE: Taylor, I'm afraid we do just that,
　　by not turning them around and back.
　　I would have you send dispatch to Davis
　　promising disaster lest we have troops.
　　I feel in a vise, not vice of sin—
　　although I think that preferable—
　　but hemmed in, sewed into small pockets.
　　We have lost many men and many boys;
　　we are at combat with a bulldog.
　　Go do it, and return yourself promptly.

(Exit Taylor)

SCENE 15

The field. A shaft of moonlight in woods. Voices. No one is seen, nothing moves. Distant, occasional, rifle fire. Summer crickets. Alternately whispered and spoken softly.

SIMON: Psst, Johnny, psst. Hey, John Reb. *(Silence)* Hey, hey. Can y'hear me? I can smell your pipe over here. *(Silence)* Can see it from time to time, too. Hey. *(Silence)* Smells good. *(Silence)* How'd you like a bullet in your bowl, John?

TOMMY: Don't, damn you, it's my only pipe.

SIMON: I got bacon for some tobacco.

TOMMY: True bacon?

SIMON: And fresh. *(Silence)* Pretty fresh.

TOMMY: I don't know now, yank, this is good tobacco. I got it day before yesterday at Harrisburg.

SIMON: Why, this bacon's off a Mississippi hog, too.

TOMMY: You keep it then, Yank. *(Silence)*

SIMON: Well, what d'you need? *(Silence)*

TOMMY: A cap. My head's cold.

SIMON: Where's yours?

TOMMY: One of you bastards made me lose it today.

SIMON: Well, ain't that a shame. *(Silence)*

TOMMY: Is it a trade?

SIMON: Can't trade a piece of uniform, Johnny, it belongs to my
   Uncle Samuel and he's only letting me use it a spell. *(Silence)*

TOMMY: Say, have you got a mess cup? I need one.

SIMON: I have. I'll throw it over. Wrap the tobacco in paper.

TOMMY: I reckon I'll have to use a sock; I haven't got any paper.
   Put a stone in the sock and throw it back.

SIMON: Here comes your cup.

TOMMY: Got it. *(Silence)* Here's your tobacco.

SIMON: *(Silence)* And here's your sock. Phew, godalmighty.
   (Silence)

TOMMY: Thanks, Yank. *(Silence)*

SIMON: Thanks, Johnny. *(Silence)* Oh, isn't that good.

TOMMY: How many of you fellows are there?

SIMON: Why, the whole Army of the Potomac. We decided to have a grand comin' out for y'. I'd say we got a good hundred thousand here, or more.

TOMMY: I reckon we've got that.

SIMON: Grant's our new commander.

TOMMY: What, another one?

SIMON: Well, you boys have been rough as hell on us.
(Silence) I'm next in line, I think. Thanks again for the tobacco, Johnny.

TOMMY: Lookit that moon—pretty.

SIMON: Peaceful, too, if those fools over yonder ever stop shootin'.

TOMMY: There's nice country 'round here. *(Silence)* What's your name, Yank?

SIMON: Simon, what's yours?

TOMMY: Tommy. Damn the war; let's go fishin', Simon.

SIMON: You're on. I'll tie some hooks, Tom.

TOMMY: No, Tommy, dammit. I'll cut me a long pole.

SIMON: Cut me one, and I'll dig the worms.

TOMMY: Two poles, comin' up.

SIMON: Night crawlers all over the ground here. Night crawlers and worms catch bass.

TOMMY: And bream.

SIMON: And perch.

TOMMY: And blue gill.

SIMON: And crappie.

TOMMY: How're you comin' with the bait?

SIMON: I'm digging now.

TOMMY: Your pole's finished; I'll cut mine.

SIMON: Then some hooks tied and we'll be off.

TOMMY: Moonlight fishing is the best in the world.

SIMON: Second to none, Tommy.

TOMMY: You like a stiff pole?

SIMON: No, but my ol' lady does, I'll tell y'. You like fat crawlers?

TOMMY: No, thin, Simon. Those fat devils get away in water.

SIMON: I nearly got enough, I think. I'll ready the hooks.

TOMMY: What a pole I found for you.

SIMON: A two-hook line for you, too, improves your chances.

TOMMY: Say, we're hung for bobbers.

SIMON: No need for them at night.

TOMMY: That's true. *(Silence)* Well, are we ready?

SIMON: That's nice. *(Silence)* Look at that moonlight.

TOMMY: It sure is lovely.

SIMON: Goodnight, Tommy.

TOMMY: 'Night Simon.

SIMON: Want to go again tomorrow night?

TOMMY: It's a date—just the two of us.

SCENE 16

Scene at night. Grant, Rawlins, Meade, and other officers. The night is quiet. Perhaps crickets can be heard, a whippoorwill. Meade and other officers enter to Grant and Rawlins already placed.

MEADE: Your pleasure, Sir.

GRANT: My pleasure is to leave Lee wondering
  where in dark heaven we have gone to.
  I want these armies out and around the James.

MEADE: Richmond, here comes your maker.

GRANT: Oh, now, Meade,
  I've not come all this way to make, but to undo.

MEADE: Nothing matters, so long as Richmond falls.

GRANT: The goal is Petersburg, somewhat south,
  not Richmond.

MEADE: Oh, Grant, I thought I knew you. So, but
  when?

GRANT: Now. Precisely now, Meade. In darkness
  and with noise no louder than the frogs.
  Close as our lines are, I want ours emptied
  and our troops night-marched to Petersburg,
  there to quickly wreck all rails to Richmond
  and lay firm siege on both those cities.

MEADE: Lee will discover us, for certain.

GRANT: Nossir, leave cavalry after you
    to ride, holler, and fire through the lines.
    March well to the rear by New Kent Church.

MEADE: It is fantastic, but I'll see to it.

GRANT: Quietly. We must not be caught. We're thieves.

MEADE: Thieves you say? Stealing what, if you don't mind?

GRANT: We are stealing a march on Mister Lee.

MEADE: History is being made, Grant.

GRANT: Good, now go.

   (Exit Meade and officers)

RAWLINS: Thieves, indeed, Sir.

SCENE 17

Scene is Cold Harbor. Lee, Taylor.

LEE: What do you mean, gone?

TAYLOR: Gone, Sir. I mean absent.

LEE: How can an army of that great size
    Be missing to us?

TAYLOR: Our own cavalry
    hit nothing but cavalry behind their lines.
    There is no infantry, few batteries.
    Not one campsite full or wagon present.
    Grant is gone.

LEE: He's stolen a march on me, then,
    and heads for Richmond. Ready all commands,
    Colonel, to march this hour. Now, Sir, now!

(Exit Colonel Taylor)

Scene 18

The scene is City Point, Grant's headquarters. Present are Grant and Meade.

GRANT: We have stretched Lee thin as we can make him,
 from Petersburg to Richmond—still he holds.
 There is one answer for it—To stretch more.
 When Lincoln goes we will take Petersburg.

MEADE: You think so?

GRANT: I believe so.

MEADE: Where is he now?

GRANT: He is reviewing General Ord's troops
 and should be here shortly. He looks bad
 a horse. Too long, too long, for these animals.
 He needs to ride a giraffe, nothing else
 shorter-legged. He discredits our mounts,
 making them look the size of burros.

MEADE It will be good to see him again.

GRANT: I'm told his wife comes separately behind.

MEADE: Thank goodness for small favors!
 If I know Ord, he has had the President
 review with Mrs. Ord. That would destroy
 Mary Lincoln. She is madly jealous.

GRANT: Really? Well, so he has, in fact. What now?

MEADE: It would be wise to call Lincoln off
    if there is danger of discovery
    by his wife. I would fear the outcome.

GRANT: Meade, are you exaggerating?!

MEADE: Not one bit.

GRANT: Lincoln is henpecked?! Moused? Harried? Preyed on?

MEADE: Lincoln is married to a very vain
    and jealous woman is all I can say.
    She has her irregularities,
    as we do.

GRANT: Damn, call Rawlins! Please. *(Calls)* Rawlins!

(Enter Rawlins)

RAWLINS: Yes, Sir.

GRANT: Escort the President here. Now!

RAWLINS: His party is approaching, Sir, the review
    is over.

GRANT: *(Much relieved)* Bless us, what unearned luck.

MEADE: Well, that scatters that cloud, Sam. His visit's saved.

GRANT: So, perhaps, is this army. *(They laugh)*

RAWLINS: I'll bring him in.

GRANT: Thank you, Colonel.

(Exit Rawlins)

No dose of that in my camp.

(Enter Rawlins)

RAWLINS: General Grant, Sir, General Meade, the President.

(Enter Lincoln, exit Rawlins)

MEADE: Mr. President, a pleasure again.

GRANT: Mr. President, how was the review?

LINCOLN: It has been a long time, General Meade.
    The review was splendid, thank you, Grant.
    The horse, though, was small. *(Grant and Meade laugh)*

GRANT: Sir, that was
    Cincinnati.

LINCOLN: Your own?

GRANT: My own.

LINCOLN: Isn't he small?

GRANT: By what
    scale, Sir?

LINCOLN: Good Lord, I do forget on occasion,
    don't I? He is a noble animal,
    then, and my apologies to him.
    Sir, I hear you have a ring in Lee's nose.

GRANT: That may be an editor's view of it
    whose job is to sell his newspapers,
    but the picture here is somewhat different.
    No one puts a ring in Mister Lee's nose,
    or elsewhere on him, lacking his consent.
    I lead a strategy he can't follow,
    he lacks both numbers and provision.
    We are thinning his defensive wall
    by stretching, mainly southward, presently.
    When he is stretched skinny, we'll go through him
    where penetration costs us the least.

LINCOLN: Then you'll have him.

GRANT: No, he will withdraw westward.
    Then I'll have him, if pursuit is sharp.

LINCOLN: It is a nasty checkerboard affair,
    in short. Jumping is important, though.

GRANT: Sir, if we should jump too high in his view
    he would shoot us down like starlings.
    I cannot conceive of playing checkers

with Lee without my finding most unpleasantly
somewhere mid-game that the call is to chess.

LINCOLN: May I see your maps?

GRANT: Most assuredly. *(Lincoln
comes round to Grant's side of the table.)*

LINCOLN: Well, who is where?

GRANT: We are everywhere.

LINCOLN: What does that signify?

GRANT: In whose hands, Sir?

LINCOLN: Why, yours.

GRANT: Sir, we'll win. Your re-election
came off handsomely, I might add now.
The people wanted you and you complied
efficiently with their warmest desires
by grooming your machine for victory.
I could never have improved your tactics.

LINCOLN: Alas, I'm being told something.

GRANT: I would never...

LINCOLN: Ah, but you would and that certifies
my confidence in you. But, for God's sake,
what of Sherman?

GRANT: Safe, I guarantee.
    These are dispatches from him.

LINCOLN: All those?

GRANT: Yes, Sir.

LINCOLN: May I read them?

GRANT: I suppose, if you have to.

LINCOLN: If I have to! No, I don't. But where is he?! *(Looking
    lost but pleased at Meade) (Pause)*

GRANT: You'd like to know?

LINCOLN: God knows, you know I would!
    But I'll not ask again. I am content
    to know that you know, if you do, I guess.

GRANT: He is detached from and free of a base
    and moves loose, living on the rebel land.
    This makes him destructive and exposed.

LINCOLN: I'll assume he is gone to Florida
    to bathe his army on the beaches there,
    and he will bask in sunlight for a while.

GRANT: That improves his safety and will enlarge
    his confidence in you, Sir.

LINCOLN: But he's safe?

GRANT: I would say it is the South that's unsafe.

LINCOLN: Well, there is but one thing troubling me, then.
   And that is: What am I to learn here?

GRANT: To trust, when things go well, that improvement's
   not impossible.

LINCOLN: This is the mixture in you that goes well,
   audacity, humility, and strength.
   You have it and you whip it constantly.
   I am reliant on you, trust you,
   and do credit you with being equal
   to him you oppose. I will not worry.
   My heaven, whose kitten is that? *(Noticing a box)*

MEADE: As far as we know, it's mother's, sir.

LINCOLN: And
   where is she?

MEADE: Dead.

LINCOLN: *(Picking the white kitten out of the box)*
   Oh, now, but you are white,
   so soft, so soft,
   and will scatter the light
   when held aloft.

   You were given for love,
   and though that's lost,
   it will return with the dove
   before next frost.

MEADE: There are two more somewhere.

LINCOLN: Well, have them found and cared for, won't you?
  (Meade goes to the door and presumably gives instructions for
  the finding and care of the cats)

GRANT: If it were a striped and homely tabby,
  would you treat it the same, Mr. Lincoln?

LINCOLN: Better, Grant. I have affinity with
  and sympathy for the ugly I defend.

GRANT: Your humanism dresses your dignity
  and the composite whole is marvelous.

LINCOLN: Why, thank you, Mr. Grant, I never thought
  a tough old beard like yourself would have thoughts
  so tender. I sincerely thank you.

MEADE: *(Returning, stonily. To Lincoln)*
  Mrs. Lincoln is with General Ord.

LINCOLN: Well, if I am not there for a while
  they will treat her like a newly crowned king.
  When I arrive, the king is present,
  and distracts from the notice given to her.
  She likes to play it solus now and then.

MEADE: However, General Ord is much embarrassed.

LINCOLN: Did she hear of my review with Mrs. Ord?

MEADE: I'm afraid so.

LINCOLN: I'm plain mortified.

MEADE: She has insulted Badeau, her guide,
  and searches out Mrs. Ord.

LINCOLN: Oh, God, Meade,
  do something. Diplomat her out of it.

MEADE: I will, Sir, rest easy.

  (Exit Meade)

GRANT: It will disappear
  and not be thought of after. Relax, Sir.

LINCOLN: I am not myself with her any more.
  Strangely, I am accused of urbane thoughts,
  mind. The flesh is weak, she says. Her Bible
  tells her so. She is like a Sunday school
  recitation. So, Sir, I have duties
  and now you know their extent. Best go help Meade,
  I think.

GRANT: Stay, Lincoln, Meade is capable.
  I share in your anxiety, your grief,
  and would allay it all, if possible.

LINCOLN: When war is done, it will continue.
  Study that.

GRANT: What causes such cleavage?

LINCOLN: We had four sons, losing two. Could it be
    that, I often think? But answer doesn't come.
    Still I must question it day and night,
    before the sun rises, Grant, after it sets,
    alone and with her, though never to her.

GRANT: It may be temporary and will right
    itself.

LINCOLN: Thank you for that pellet of hope;
    I will pocket it in this old coat
    and go dressed to my bed this evening.
    It is not a soft thing like kitty here
    and not light, but perhaps I can live with it.
    Our position in this war is providence
    to me now. Let the thing be pressed hard.

GRANT: I will. And since I am well decided
    that this army shall be Lee's vanquisher,
    you may predict it to your cabinet.

LINCOLN: But what if Sherman should reach Lee first?

GRANT: He won't.

LINCOLN: But what if—I see. I see.

GRANT: It would balance with the Western armies
    if this Eastern one should close the conflict.

LINCOLN: You may make a politician someday.

GRANT: After you, Sir, after you. Long after.

LINCOLN: Well, it is time for me. I must retire.

GRANT: You have my strictest confidence, Sir,
    in all our matters and my best wishes.
    I will try to take this conflict off your back
    in short time.

LINCOLN: *(Standing)* God bless you, General Grant.

GRANT: The kitten?

LINCOLN: Oh, can't you make a place for her?

GRANT: I promise the cook to care for them.

LINCOLN: I am much obliged in all directions.
    (Sets the cat back in her box)

GRANT: *(Shakes his hand)*
    A safe and pleasant return to you
    and Mrs. Lincoln.

LINCOLN: Bless you, Grant.

GRANT: Rawlins!

    (Enter Rawlins)

Please escort Mr. President, Sir.

LINCOLN: Bless, Sir. *(Grant salutes)*

(Exit Lincoln and Rawlins)

GRANT: *(To himself)* I would wager my soul on that man.
  (Looks at the kitten in the box.)
  Kitty, kitty, kitty.

(Enter Meade)

MEADE: I beg your pardon?

GRANT: Nothing, Meade, come in.

MEADE: It was sad.

GRANT: Here, too.

MEADE: It was like another war within a war.

GRANT: And there sat the worn defender of it all:
  of nation, home, morality, and self.

MEADE: With his kitten.

GRANT: True, with his kitten.
  Let's go. When it's over we'll get drunk together.

SCENE 19

Scene outside Richmond, Lee's camp. Lee and Taylor. Distant cannon, close musket.

LEE: We are ragged, sick, and stretched too thin.

TAYLOR: And outnumbered.

LEE: Oh, well, that's nothing new.
    If only we could turn them somewhere.

TAYLOR: Turn
    them, you say!

LEE: Yes, get around them somewhere.

TAYLOR: But we have barely enough men to set
    in front of them. Where are the others?

LEE: A remnant of Hood's old corps, perhaps.

TAYLOR: Hood was destroyed by Thomas, left behind
    by Sherman at Atlanta. He was broken
    at Nashville.

LEE: There must be pieces left.

TAYLOR: No Sir, Thomas leaves no pieces, no shards.
    Hood was not routed, beaten, or repulsed.
    He was run over and destroyed, all in all.
    There's no more of him.

LEE: My head of steam gone,
    Go to Davis now and tell him, say
    we'll need provision at Amelia Court House,
    not far from Richmond. That's where we go next.
    And tell him, reflect on Agamemnon.

TAYLOR: I will, Sir. Withdraw, if you will now,
    to the inner line.

LEE: Is this the outer?

TAYLOR: Yessir, and those are blue coats on that hill
    Yonder.

LEE: I will. Now off with you, Taylor.

SCENE 20

In the field beyond Amelia. Grant and Meade. Rifle fire.

(Enter Meade)

MEADE: I'm at arm's length from Lee.

GRANT: Close is in his beard,
   Meade!

MEADE: I'll have to hit his General Ewell,
   then. That officer is between us
   in undetermined strength.

GRANT: Do you know what
   I would do?

MEADE: I'm rather sure I do, Sam.

GRANT: Determine, hit, and erase Ewell.

MEADE: I was right.

GRANT: Well, good. Then learn it and hit Ewell.

MEADE: I've both learned it and hit him already;
   I am at arm's length from Lee.

GRANT: In his beard?!

MEADE: Or in his beard.

GRANT: Oh, Meade, ignore my nerves;
    I want it done, is all, done and over.
    Then the fox is hurting, and most likely
    is stalled afield. I'll send him an overture
    toward peace and see what his first rejection
    will be made of. It's due and finished.
    Good Meade, you have fulfilled. Let me attempt
    as well on paper.

(Exit Meade)

SCENE 21

Lee afield. Taylor and other officers present. Distant, close musketry.

TAYLOR: Some officers have thought, with all respect,
   and heads together, about surrender, Sir.

LEE: Pity no good thoughts came of all those heads.

TAYLOR: They wished to save you embarrassment, I'm sure.

LEE: Embarrassment is not my great pain, Sir,
   losing is that.

TAYLOR: Is there wisdom in quitting?

LEE: There is hollow defeat in it, surely.

TAYLOR: Sir, will you come to this knoll above me?
   There is a view here of Ewell's army,
   with which you've had no contact for a day.

LEE: Why, gladly, I never knew he was so close.
   Why can't I contact him? Is he lost?
   The strength of Ewell is important to us.
   Who are those men below?

TAYLOR: Stragglers, wounded,
   defeated, or deserters, Sir.

LEE: My God.

TAYLOR: Then there's this from the Federal lines, Sir.
   Their courier waits. *(Hands a message to Lee)*

LEE: *(Reads)*   Tell me what you think.

TAYLOR: General, your decision is mine.

LEE: I
   think it time.

   (Exit Taylor)

SCENE 22

Scene is the White House. Present are Seward and Stanton. Bells tolling, diminishing.

SEWARD: Regardez, Stanton, the war is ended.
  Think about it, taste it, sit on it,
  rub it in but hardly doubt it. It's done.
  An old courthouse witnessed ultimate law.

STANTON: Oh, Seward, it's marvelous that it's done.

SEWARD: Arms were stacked. Then from the house, terms given
  and terms accepted, some said a dove flew
  while others called the bird a brown thrasher.
  Is there a difference? I'm in politics.

STANTON: Whatever the bird, one thing is sure:
  it was put to flight by fear of all that brass
  in one small room, I can promise you.

SEWARD: It's done. My wife reduced herself to tears
  on hearing the news from your good wife.
  Where is Lincoln now?

STANTON: Upstairs, alone
  with his joy, where he's been for an hour.

SEWARD: *(At a window)* There are people out there waiting to
  hear from him. And they're an ecstatic crowd.

STANTON: Yet, Seward, will they bind to our new role?
    The purpose of an aggregate nation
    is not segregation or separate
    entities anymore than marriage
    is composed of a divided housing.
    These States United, these several states,
    of mountain, plain, swamp, of farm, and township,
    so diverse and lovely in their aspect,
    so green, so emblazoned by western sun,
    have fought and died for conjunction, a knot
    making us all parts of an embodied whole.

SEWARD: Peace is like the homing of a lost dog.
    Something they dearly loved is now restored.

STANTON: And will remain at peace until next war.

(Enter Lincoln)

LINCOLN: My good Seward, you look fine in peacetime.

SEWARD: Look, Stanton, he's suffused with happiness.

STANTON: What to do with the renegade Davis?

LINCOLN: I hope he's safe. Davis did no more wrong
    than pilot his belief, which Lee did, too.

SEWARD: But he's the pack leader.

LINCOLN: We've sunk the ship,

Seward, must we sink after it to heap
disfiguration on disablement
by knifing away at her figurehead?
The pack dispersed has no rightful leader.

SEWARD: True enough. I believe this is the sane course.

LINCOLN: I know it is. I furthermore think Grant
   did more wisely with a soft hand than fist
   would do. So I commend his downy terms.
   The man, for me, was born a winner
   who, deprived of opposition, falters
   but who, when pressed with it, will activate
   and bristle to battle. He knows both hard
   and tender disposition and commands
   himself in these. He is all we've needed
   these four years. He lacks ostentation,
   color and show, but notes in black and white
   job to be done and job done moves on.
   We are fortunate in having him.

SEWARD: *(At the window)*
   Will you put food in these hungry mouths? They
   gape for something.

LINCOLN: One hour ago I told them
   God had at last granted us victory
   and thought the pun would knock them laughing
   back to their homes, to church or, at very least
   to taverns. I can't address them any more.

SEWARD: I'll excuse myself to duty. Good health,
   Lincoln.

LINCOLN: Bless you, Seward. To yours, also.

(Exit Seward)

LINCOLN: Stanton, there is some noting a bird's flight
    to the outdoors from a high rafter
    once papers were signed and accord gained;
    could it have been a vulture with a full crop,
    d'you think, well fed but disgusted with men
    and the costs of their politics, tell me.

STANTON: Who cares? I can tell you it was lucky
    to get out of there at all in good health.
    Lee's long sword could have taken a wing off
    from sheer frustration, humiliated.

LINCOLN: Well, then, here ends our ornithology
    and our satire and here begins the joy
    we've been deprived of since my first investment
    of office, first barkload of pink children
    charged with making steady a stricken ship.

STANTON: Right, you may call me that.

LINCOLN: I think I have.
    Now, however be the color of joy,
    whatever that may be, my good Stanton,
    we have survived. The sun paints the sky blue
    again and life's prospects can be greater
    than sudden death. It's a time to cast smiles
    on one another, beat drums, castanets

and give over any thought of anger
to our once and now new citizens.
I want to say I love all men again
as though I'd not always executed that.
Be that as it may, I breathe deeper now.
I swell with a zest for things, an ardor
now for managing a nation back to health,
to life and to union. It's not meant
we divide. Now look on the bloody proof;
never meant, never will mean. We're greatness
whole, these states, these great United States.
Do my patriotics embarrass you?

STANTON: Sir, I am just so tired from the times' work
　　　that turning my mouth's corners up in smile
　　　seems blasphemous to earth's gravity. It's
　　　a tug I'm losing.

LINCOLN:　　　　　Will you help me now?

STANTON: Do I quit the sport for winning one game?

LINCOLN: Stanton, I am mindful for a moment
　　　of a scene I found myself player to
　　　some four years back, before inauguration.
　　　It occurred on the avenue below
　　　some little distance still from the White House.
　　　My carriage was moving in procession
　　　at its side, and stuck to it, appeared a boy.
　　　He shook my hand, beamed a golden face
　　　at me, gave me his name as Thomas Dyer,
　　　and exclaimed his happiness to meet me.

I died. He could have been an assassin
to all within. Then agents plucked him off.
I wonder now if he survived this war
or fell in it and who were his good parents.
Thomas Dyer,'he said, and could have hit me
with a shot, no aim necessary
and no miss possible. But he was friend,
not foe.

STANTON: No more of this. Assassination
is dementia praecox flowered. It brings,
in its expansion, bad air. Avoid it.

LINCOLN: I try.

STANTON: Well, succeed, Lincoln. Do succeed.

LINCOLN: I have had a dream.

STANTON: Forget you had it.

LINCOLN: Why, if I cut my hand, would you tell me,
    forget it?

STANTON: I would do the best thing for you
    as I have just done.

(Enter Mary Lincoln opposite, exit Stanton)

MARY: I've looked for you, Abe.
    But I looked in all the empty places first.

LINCOLN: *(Smiling, but growing again serious)*
I'm quite surprised I wasn't there.

MARY: How so?

LINCOLN: You said an empty place.

MARY: What bothers you, Abe?
I haven't loved you all these slow years
to be so readily confused, Sir.

LINCOLN: It is a dream, Mary, a shabby dream.

MARY: Tell it to me, Abe.

LINCOLN: So, I will, then.
The thing will lean on my imprisoned mind
'til sense collapses. Some ten days ago,
going late to bed, I fell aslumber
quickly from the long day behind and dreamt
in terrifying realness of a sound.
This note, diminished as it was, held forth
against a background of gigantic stillness.
This relieved to sounds of sobbing and grief,
mute and distant, tremulous but subdued.
I thought I left my bed, wandered downstairs,
heard the crying louder than before,
but saw not a soul. The stillness returned
and rooms seemed three times larger than real size.
Vast was everything! Vast! The sobbing, then,
seemed to tear the walls as I approached

their proper amplitude, and I grew fearful.
I came here to this room, which I entered.
And its sight did sicken me, there, to behold
a damned catafalque with corpse laid out
in funeral vestments, soldiers around it
posted, and mourners paying choked homage
to its hooded face. Who's in there, I cried?!
Who is dead in the White House?! I demanded,
of a soldier. My God, so slow to speak!
Then he turned and answered, The President,
he was killed by an assassin!—To me!
This was addressed to me! A chorus of woe
from the mourners woke me and I slept no more
that night. And this is the dream that plagues me
no small bit of late. It chews on me.   '

MARY: That is horrid, I wish you had not told it.

LINCOLN: Well, it's only a dream. I'll say no more
    about it. I shouldn't have frightened you
    with it and will atone by taking you
    to some play tonight somewhere, or something.

MARY: Oh, Abe, I would enjoy that!

LINCOLN: Get ready, then.

MARY: And, Sir, since I love you, I will have the cook
    put up a feast of your favorite foods,
    and will dress for dinner. This in love
    and my affection. It is Good Friday, Abe.

LINCOLN: Why, so it is.

(Exit Mary Lincoln)

LINCOLN: Ah, now it's to a show
   to see illusion in another key.

*(Enter Elizabeth Keckley, Mulatto, dressmaker and assistant to Mary
Lincoln)*

ELIZABETH: I thought Mrs. Lincoln was here, Sir.

LINCOLN: You were right when you thought so, Elizabeth.
   She was. Mrs. Lincoln went to dress.

ELIZABETH: I'll join her, then. She will want my help.

LINCOLN: No, do join me first a moment, if you will.
   I have a question of you. More, perhaps,
   than the one. What store do you put in dreams?

ELIZABETH: Much importance, Sir.

LINCOLN: Well, you are agnostic
   and accredit dreams? How's that?

ELIZABETH: I never knew
   the two to be connected, Mr. President.

LINCOLN: That's well answered. Well, then, how is reason
   made of dreaming, tell me?

ELIZABETH: I don't know, Sir.
    I can tell you how dreams occurred to me,
    and coming true—

LINCOLN: No, no, none of that.
    They are too specific to be of value.
    Do they foretell?

ELIZABETH: Oh, yes, sometimes they do.

LINCOLN: Well, regularly or not?

ELIZABETH: Quite so, Sir.

LINCOLN: I can't believe it. I will wish not to.

ELIZABETH: Don't, Sir, do not believe it. Give it up.
    I have surmised the dream is no good,
    forget it. Close the window of your mind
    and stifle the experience. I live
    with dreams as I would with any poor game
    played by poor folks—more for their entertainment
    than their truth. Therefore, I can't explain it.

LINCOLN: Now, that is a just account embracing truth.
    It makes me easy. I have come closer
    to my God these last years, while you have not.
    How do you fare?

ELIZABETH: Well, Sir.

LINCOLN: Do you fear dreams?

ELIZABETH: With cause, yes.

LINCOLN: Here is no cause, and there's our rift.

ELIZABETH: Sir, you would, without cause, fear anything
    that would threaten your serenity.
    But we are all happy with you here.

LINCOLN: Here is not everywhere, Elizabeth.

ELIZABETH: Nowhere is everywhere. But more approve
    than disapprove. You are in the hands, still,
    of your majority. Your conscience
    is clear on that point, surely, is it not?

LINCOLN: Yes, and every other that I know.
    But it is God, Madam, not my conscience
    that has buffered me against my dream.
    Conscience is weak and too susceptible.

ELIZABETH: Well, I admire your protection, Sir,
    and envy it.

LINCOLN: I need it. I do need it.
    Tell me now, how will Negro people
    use their freedom? It's a new thing to them.

ELIZABETH: You have freed them from slavery physically,
    Mr. President. Now you or someone
    or time must free them from it mentally.
    Recovery resides in performance, Sir.

LINCOLN: That's true, and should be recorded of me.
Well, I won't keep you.

ELIZABETH: The dream is harmless,
Sir. I hope you lose it.

LINCOLN: Well, I thank you.

ELIZABETH: And—

LINCOLN: I think you'd best attend Mrs. Lincoln, now.

ELIZABETH: Bless you, Sir.

LINCOLN: And have Him keep me, thank you.

(Exit Elizabeth. Enter Mary opposite)

MARY: There is a rebel actor in the house
and he's armed, I hear.

LINCOLN: And so the play now?!
Is it I who am nakedly on stage,
an actor from an alleyway, a stand-in,
mumbling his last lines to an empty house?
Mary, you had better take refuge now.

MARY: Yes, so, Abe. But the actor will be caught
and handled. Why all this negative talk?

(Enter Elizabeth)

ELIZABETH: I was told you had returned, Mrs. Lincoln.

MARY: Yes, although I hardly know why, I did.

(Enter Stanton opposite)

STANTON: Sir, there is Seward's blood on every wall
    of his house! A young rebel maniac
    purged him with a damn knife so many times
    he's near death! What's more, there's an actor here
    in this house with the same lethal intent!
    Murder ups the ante for the vanquished.
    Lincoln, you're in danger!

LINCOLN: I will be out
    shortly, however. Either you will find him
    or he will find me.

STANTON: The latter follows
    in this room, I fear. The police have lost him.

LINCOLN: There was a time when I felt alien
    to the White House but I am history here
    now and honor it most unguardedly.
    I cannot run in my own house, Stanton.
    I am at peace with myself at any cost.

STANTON: Please hear me, Lincoln, security's gone.

LINCOLN: The ladies might be let out, don't you think?

STANTON: I swear I don't know.

ELIZABETH: Oh, do beware, Sir,
    the dream is coming about like a giant ship
    against weak moorings.

MARY: Elizabeth, no!

ELIZABETH: Oh, yes, Ma'm, yes. It is the occurrence,
    I fear, of a dream in reality
    and to this moment is dedicated!
    We have discussed it.

MARY: Mere rubbish and rot!

LINCOLN: Oh, find a cave for them to hang in, Stanton.

STANTON: Ladies, for safety's sake follow me.

MARY: I will not be kept at arm's length, Abe.

ELIZABETH: He is preparing himself, Mrs. Lincoln.

MARY: And for what, you foolish woman, for what?!

ELIZABETH: For peace, Ma'm, for lasting peace.

LINCOLN: The dream's on me,
    and I have unknown minutes, not hours.
    But if the price of peace is already paid,
    who comes late in the name of collection?
    But logic is for the courts, I know.

ELIZABETH: And understanding for the halls of life.
Man is man, Mr. President.

LINCOLN: Ah, yes,
and the leases we have on life are short,
Madam, especially when hoped longer.
I had wished to pilot us a while more.

STANTON: Lincoln, another room. The library.

LINCOLN: Read, Stanton? We have done that for ages. *(The shadow of a gunman falls upstage.)*

MARY: Oh, my god, my God!
(A shot and Lincoln slumps forward. The shadow disappears)
They have shot him! They have killed my husband!

(Enter two Pinkerton men, armed)

STANTON: *(To the two men)* The gunman is off there. Take him either way.

(Exit the two men)

ELIZABETH: Now they will find the abject assassin. *(On inspecting Lincoln)*
The murderer has caused a mortal blow
and doctors will probe, then do nothing.
It is the end of time, my President.

MARY: Oh, Abe, Abe, my light, my path, my shadow

brightened, my advantage, my fruition
in a life choked to standstill and madness.
Grey skies hang overhead like unwashed sheets
and April is autumn. Oh, dear Abe,
the wars, all the wars, conclude together
and my Jupiter lies drained and broken.

STANTON: Such a loathsome show of hollow strength,
    this act, and it descends upon us hard.
    He was a peaceful lamb in puma's coat,
    dove who mocked the form of swiftest merlin,
    a treasure too completely uninsured
    in flesh to shield him against the bullet
    of a fancied martyr. It is death now
    for him and darkness and our lights grow dim
    awhile, too, candle to candle, flame to flame.
    Then, and only after then, shall our lives
    bear the lovely fruits of hallowed meaning.
    Goodnights be said to him, he is passing on.

(Closing Lincoln's lids)

He was alone among us, and is now.

THE END

0-595-74516-4

Printed in the United States
903800002B